Tectonic signifies the fusion of technique with art, of construction with poetry.

The radical tectonic is a vital sign, emerging evidence of the watchful eye and the trace of the hand in architecture.

Challenging the commodification and standardization of building production, the radical tectonic reaches beyond the merely pragmatic.

The radical not accept the conjunction programme. it reflects of changing evolving social and the hybrid of institutions.

tectonic does
idealized
of form and
Instead,
the reality
technologies,
patterns
increasingly
character

The renewed interest in the tectonic is an affirmation that the making of the physical artifact *is* radical, that it is at the centre of architectural discourse and rooted in craft, culture and context.

In addition to the enhancement of individual experience, this architecture is directed toward the creation of shared social landscapes: rather than being an esoteric private dialect of the élite, the richly expressive language of the art of construction is firmly engaged in the public realm.

The radical tectonic finds its expression in the physical and material attributes of construction, enhancing the body's experience of space and incorporating sophisticated and sustainable technologies.

Radical
Tectonics

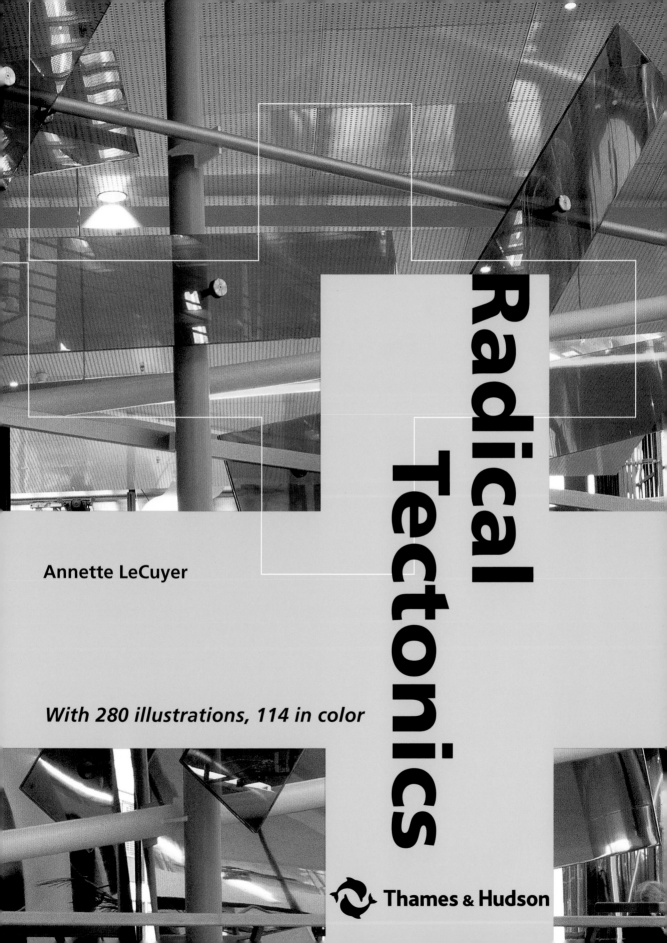

Annette LeCuyer

With 280 illustrations, 114 in color

Radical Tectonics

Thames & Hudson

3.21

3.22

3.23

3.24

3.11

3.12

3.13

3.14

mecanoo

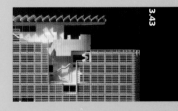

patkau architects

3.00 Summer House, Muuratsalo, Finland, 1953
Many modernist architects have been preoccupied with industrialized systems of mass production. Alvar Aalto, conversely, sought to humanize modernism by exploring the expressive potential of material and transforming constructional necessity into poetry, as exemplified by the idiosyncratic nature of the brick wall of his summer house.

Introduction

Radical Tectonics:
Making and Meaning

Tectonic – derived from the Greek word *tekton*, meaning carpenter or builder – signifies the fusion of technique with art, of construction with poetry. Although widely used by architects today, it is a term that seems strangely at odds with the reality of much contemporary building. Tectonic suggests a preoccupation with materiality and a championing of craft that respect the trace of the hand and the expressive potential of construction. Current practice, however, is increasingly concerned with more generalized buildings that are constructed, both physically and metaphorically, at greater distances from the architects who design them. As the production of the built artifact has evolved from craft-based fabrication to the assembly of mass-produced, standardized components, so the reality of the modernist quest for the universal detail has proved to be less compelling than the idea. Buildings have become homogenized, divorced from the contingencies of craft and culture. Emphasizing technique at the expense of art, the delicate equilibrium implicit in the term tectonic has been undermined.

The radical tectonic may be seen as a form of resistance that attempts to restore the balance. By challenging the commodification and standardization of building production, a number of architects have explored ways in which construction can reach beyond the merely pragmatic. The work of Alvar Aalto – noteworthy for its humanization of modernism through a 'methodical accommodation to circumstance',[1] its emphasis upon the expressive potential of material and its transformation of constructional necessity into poetry – is emblematic in this regard. Many strategies of opposition are now being energetically pursued by an ever-growing number of architects. In contrast with the current fascination with the virtual and the tendency of architecture to look to other disciplines for theoretical

3.00 Olympic Stadium, Munich, 1972
The design of the grounds and buildings for the Olympic Games in Germany signalled a dramatic change from the highly ordered systems-built projects of Günter Behnisch's early work to more expressive and complex geometries. In his later work, the overlay of multiple ordering systems signifies the importance of individual freedom in pluralist democracies.

underpinnings, the renewed interest in the tectonic is an affirmation that the making of the physical artifact *is* radical, that it is at the centre of architectural discourse and rooted in craft, culture and context. Thus, the art of construction is revealed once again as a richly expressive language through which experience and meaning are communicated.

The radical tectonic is not a style but a sensibility, a way of working with many possible manifestations. Rather than a comprehensive or coherent school of thought, the work of these four architects represents distinct approaches that have been shaped by significantly different physical and cultural conditions. The buildings and projects have been chosen for the clear way in which they embody particular tectonic issues, demonstrating both the continuity of ideas from project to project and how those ideas develop and change. However, although the tectonic languages of these architects vary, there are a number of common themes in their work.

Rejecting the ideal in favour of the real, the radical tectonic takes a critical stance with regard to typology. Instead of accepting the idealized conjunction of form and programme, building types are reconfigured to reflect the reality of changing technologies, evolving social patterns and the increasingly hybrid character of institutions. Simple, rational geometries are replaced by complex, variable and non-rational systems; the absolute becomes contingent and the paradigm inflected. While this transition is most pronounced in the long career of Günter Behnisch, it is also obvious in the design development of a single building, for instance, Mecanoo's

Library at Delft University of Technology. In the original scheme, the body of the building was a simple triangle, but the library has become a freer, more fluid form in plan and section, which provides a counterpoint to the pure cone and to the idealized symmetry of the adjacent building. A similar evolution is evident from the unifying orthogonal grid of Patkau Architects' Seabird Island School to the relaxed order of Strawberry Vale School and, in the work of Enric Miralles, from the bilateral symmetry of the seating plan for the Sports Centre at Huesca to the asymmetrical irregularity of the seating at the National Training Centre for Rhythmic Gymnastics in Alicante.

In lieu of being idealized objects superimposed on the land, these buildings grow out of the land, being shaped by and amplifying the topography of their sites. Blurring the boundaries between site and built form, they connect the architectural definition of tectonic with the branch of science that studies changes to the structure of the earth's crust. However, the term 'topographical' embodies much more than an architectural registration of the natural attributes of the terrain. These buildings aspire to be deeply contextual, like divining rods, revealing intrinsic, invisible energies

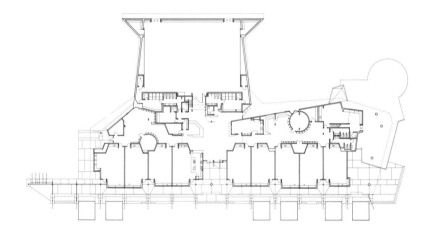

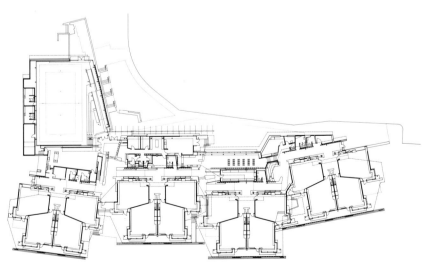

3.00 Seabird Island School, Agassiz, British Columbia, 1988–91 [top]
Strawberry Vale School, Victoria, British Columbia, 1992–96 [bottom]
In contrast with the idealized order of the grid that underpins Patkau Architects' Seabird Island School, the more informal organization of their later Strawberry Vale School adjusts to and becomes an extension of the site's natural topography.

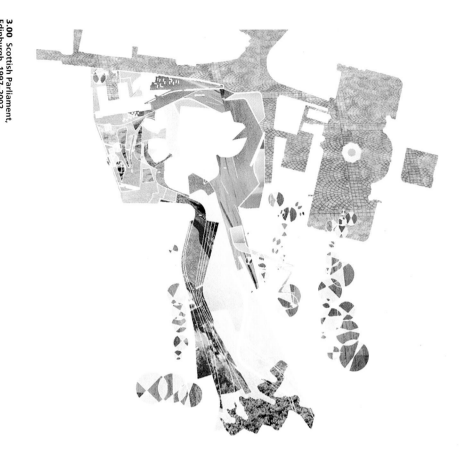

3.00 Scottish Parliament, Edinburgh, 1997–2002
In the work of Enric Miralles, collage is used as a design tool to map the interactive relationship between buildings and their physical and cultural context. As opposed to the imagined perfection of the ideal, the conflicting conditions of the real become the source of Miralles's tectonic language.

that are latent in their sites and the dynamics of their use. Instead of the erasure implied by the tabula rasa, the peculiar, conflicting and unresolved conditions of the real are embraced as the prime generators of form, space and tectonic detail. The projects grow out of meticulous readings of the ground, a rigorous mapping of imprints, rhythms, traces and tendencies, which emerge to shape what William Curtis calls 'a social landscape in which institutions, context and nature are cast in an interactive relationship'.[2] Although Curtis is referring specifically to the work of Miralles, his description might also explain the other architects' approaches – the *Situationsarchitektur* of Behnisch, the Patkaus' 'investigations into the particular' and the 'conversation with the situation' that characterizes Mecanoo's reflective mode of practice.[3] These strategies, as well as providing a rich conceptual foundation for design, acknowledge that the ideal plan is rarely realized and absorb the unpredictable and inevitable changes inherent in the process of design and construction.

A corollary of rejecting the ideal is that, as a building becomes topographical, it reads less clearly as a figural whole and more as fragments in a field of forces. The disembodiment of the building may be achieved in a number of ways: finite systems of order are replaced by open-ended and changeable systems; the monolithic gives way to the multilayered; and homogeneity is superseded by differentiation. As figure dissolves into field, the buildings are comprehended less through fixed perspective and more through the unfolding, internalized experience of the body moving through space. The architectural promenade is emphasized tectonically as the locus of heightened bodily experience. Although perspective no longer orders perception, the eye continues to play a crucial role. The view is fragmented, simultaneously focusing near and far or assembling spatial sequences as a series of partial glimpses. In addition to the visual, much importance in this work is placed upon the tactile. The construction palettes of these buildings are rich and varied, with materials used as much for their sensate qualities as for economy or utility. Like the brutalist affinity for the power of raw material, the juxtaposition of rough and smooth, heavy and light, figured and plain makes the bodily experience of the buildings more direct and more complex, supplanting objectivity with empathy.

This renewed interest in the sensate, expressed through materiality, is in turn stimulating the reintegration of craft in the building process. The radical tectonic is not a latter-day Arts and Crafts movement that repudiates the materials and processes of industrialized building production in favour of the handmade. Instead, the craft arises out of an understanding of the imperatives of contemporary materials and construction systems and the manipulation of these imperatives to more humane ends. Although the frame and thin-skin vocabulary of twentieth-century architecture – succinctly summarized by Le Corbusier's Maison Dom-ino – has sponsored many technological advances, it has also tended to define architecture in reductive terms as an ever-thinner assemblage of layers. While many bemoan this state of affairs suggesting that substance has been replaced by veneer, each of these architects has found ways of transforming this perceived liability into a virtue. Craft emerges not through the design of purpose-made systems, but rather through the layering of standard systems in unconventional ways; through revealing interstitial layers of construction that are normally hidden from view; or through the play between repetition and variation. In contrast with the detached minimalism inherent in the Maison Dom-ino – the pure abstraction of linear frame and planar slab together with the immateriality of the glazed curtain wall – the radical tectonic finds its expression in the physical and material attributes of construction. Frame and skin become highly articulated, complex entities that register the topographical forces at work, enhance the physical experience of space and incorporate sophisticated and sustainable technologies. Abandoning the ideal of immateriality, the skin becomes once again a palpable mediator between man and nature.

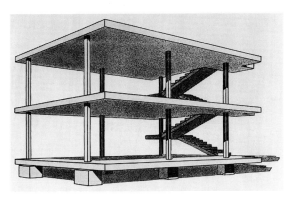

3.00 Philharmonic Hall, Berlin, 1956–63 [left]
National Gallery, Berlin, 1962–68 [right]
The idealized form and systematic order of the gallery by Mies van der Rohe are sharply juxtaposed with the more contingent, intuitive topographical form of the nearby Philharmonic Hall by Hans Scharoun. Both approaches are evident in the work of Günter Behnisch.

The importance of the physical inevitably engenders a preoccupation with construction detail, not merely as a technical task but as a vehicle for expression. Far removed from the universal detail, the complex, contingent, formal languages and material palettes of the buildings generate a rich range of spaces and a bewilderingly intricate array of junctions, each of which must be individually resolved. The detail, rather than being systematic and self-referential in its adoration of technology, becomes empathetic, evidence of the hand and mind inflecting construction conventions toward particular conceptual ends.

Creative undermining of the tyranny of industry may largely be an act of will on the part of these particular architects. However, fundamental changes in the techniques of building production bode well for the resistance movement. The computerization of manufacturing technology, although having the potential to act as an instrument of still further standardization, can be used to opposite ends. Because fabrication is increasingly digitally controlled, variation of the detail – once prohibitively costly – is now more economically viable, making small batch and even one-off production feasible. In place of the rigid macro-scale mass production that dominated the construction industry in the twentieth century, the elastic standardization espoused by Alvar Aalto – which is described as 'so varied and small in scale as to be capable of responding to the most minute concern'[4] – is now technologically possible. Manufacturers can be adaptable and, as a consequence, architects suddenly have the opportunity to shape industrial processes of fabrication. Although unable to predict the technology that would bring about this transformation, Eliel Saarinen (1873–1950), whose work also focused upon issues of craft and industry, was prescient when he suggested 'undoubtedly, mechanization of mind will turn – when the time is ripe – into humanization of the mechanized mind. Form is bound to follow the same metamorphosis.'[5]

The reintegration of craft with industry makes it possible to move beyond necessity, beyond the mere technical imperatives of construction to explore once again its expressive and representational potential. Distancing itself both from the abstraction of modernism and the overt signs and symbols of postmodernism, the radical tectonic looks to the construction itself – shaped by craft, culture and context – as the source of its iconography. By being thus rooted, it aspires to be local, yet to avoid being parochial. So while the work represented here responds to context and climate and, to a certain extent, makes use of indigenous materials and construction skills, it does so without nostalgia for a vernacular past. Instead, it is hard-headed and pragmatic, embracing the ubiquitous products and processes of industrialized building systems as the source of its expression. The sensitivity of the radical tectonic to the local is now under scrutiny. While these architects have developed particular tectonic inflections refined through a careful reading of their own land and culture, each now has projects abroad, and the degree to which the work registers the same resonance beyond its native terrain is now in the process of being tested.

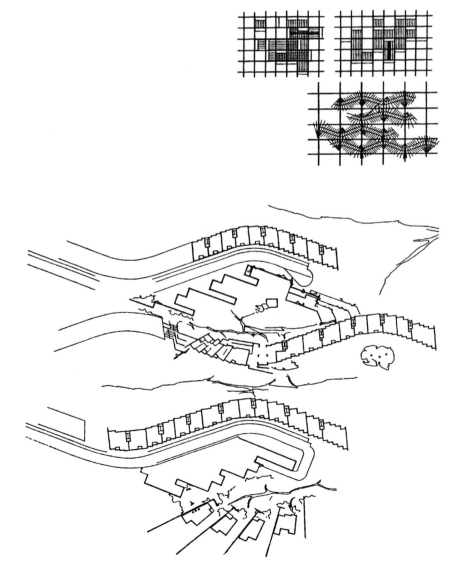

3.00 Housing, Pavia, Italy, 1966
In place of absolute standardization, Alvar Aalto advocated elastic standardization. The repetitive unit, in this site plan for a housing development in Italy, is aggregated loosely to conform to the topography of the site and to generate a variety in placement and outlook. In this way, Aalto attempted to reflect the order of nature.

Although the work of these four architects moves away from the formal, material and technological mandates of modernism, it does hold onto the social idealism that underpinned twentieth-century architecture. Their careers have been nurtured in nations strongly committed to social democracy and the projects presented here are predominantly public buildings commissioned by public entities. In addition to the enhancement of individual experience, the architecture is directed toward the creation of shared social landscapes. Rather than being an esoteric private dialect of the élite, the richly expressive language of the art of construction is firmly engaged in the public realm.

These projects, by architects who are actively being sought out to design buildings of international significance, confirm that the poetry of construction is fertile territory worthy of more intensive exploration. The radical tectonic is a creative and focused response to issues of anonymity and facelessness in today's culture. It represents a challenge to the authority of commerce as patron of architecture and the universal monotony sponsored by the industries of media and entertainment. It values the capacity of the individual to invent and build empathetically within our physical and cultural environment. The radical tectonic is a vital sign, emerging evidence of the watchful eye and the trace of the hand in architecture.

3.00 Library Delft University of Technology, 1992–97
In the work of Mecanoo, the term landscape is both literal and metaphoric. It refers to natural topographies that are amplified by the form and tectonic details of buildings, and suggests that buildings are social landscapes that shape and are shaped by human interaction.

Notes

1   Stanford Anderson. 'Aalto and "Methodical Accommodation to Circumstance"' in *Alvar Aalto in Seven Buildings* (Helsinki: Museum of Finnish Architecture, 1998) pp. 143–49.

2   William J.R. Curtis. 'Mental Maps and Social Landscapes: The Architecture of Miralles and Pinós' *El Croquis*, (no 49-50, June–September 1991) p 7.

3   Donald A. Schon. *The Design Studio: An Exploration of its Traditions and Potentials* (London: RIBA Publications Limited, 1985) p 26.

4   Edward R. Ford. *The Details of Modern Architecture, vol 2, 1928–88* (Cambridge, Massachusetts and London, England: The MIT Press, 1998) pp. 119, 145.

5   Eliel Saarinen. *The Search for Form in Art and Architecture* (New York: Dover Publications, Inc., 1985) p 323. Work first published by the Reinhold Publishing Corporation, New York (1948) under the title *Search for Form: A Fundamental Approach to Art*.

3.00 Sacello wall, Museo di Castelvecchio, Verona, Italy, 1956–73
Carlo Scarpa's design for this external wall, with its rich tapestry of texture and colour, focuses upon the sensory qualities of the materials to heighten direct corporeal experience. Scarpa also explores the potential for variation within a simple, repetitive ordering system.

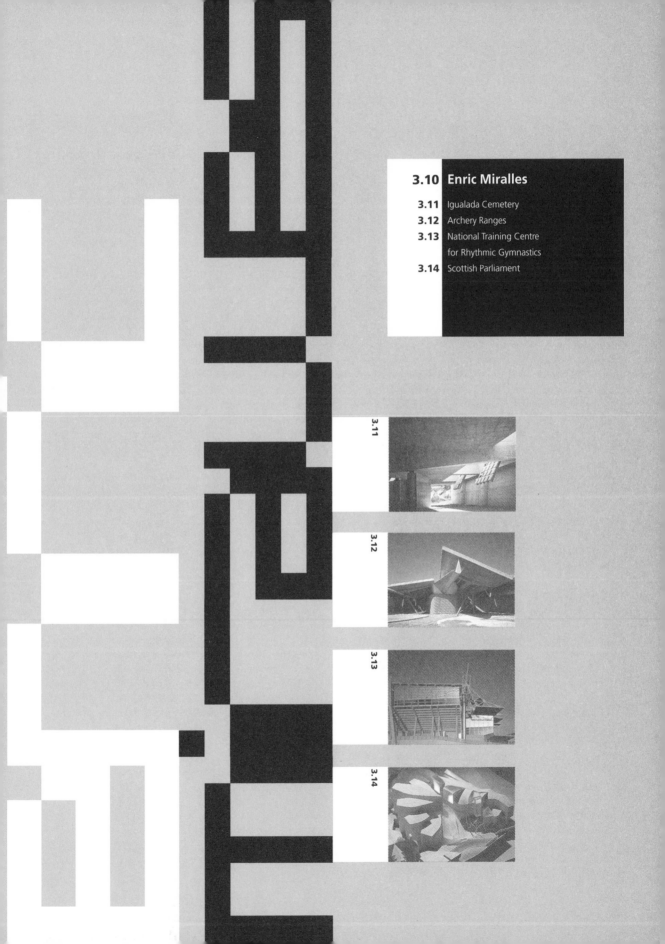

3.11

3.12

3.13

3.14

Enric Miralles
Precarious Balance

The work of Enric Miralles, formerly in association with Carme Pinós and from 1993 to 2000 with Benedetta Tagliabue, emerged out of the rebuilding of Catalonia's cultural identity following the death of Francisco Franco (1892–1975). Since 1975, an extensive programme of public works sponsored by enlightened political leadership has enabled the region's architecture to flourish. In comparison with an approach that focuses on iconic monumental buildings, the Catalan strategy has been to commission many small projects. Successful competition entries for modest interventions in public urban spaces followed by schools, town halls and other civic buildings – culminating in work for the 1992 Olympic Games in Barcelona, marking the worldwide celebration of Catalonia's rebirth – provided Miralles with a basis for the development of a tectonic language that, before his death, was being turned to larger and more complex commissions in Spain and abroad.

Early projects on residual sites at the edges of towns and cities proved to be excellent vehicles for the development of a contingent formal language that fuses landscape with building and nature with culture. A persistent theme in his early work is the duality between carved and constructed space, between what Gottfried Semper defines as stereotomic form, or earthwork, and framework. In a number of projects, stereotomic form extends far beyond the actual limits of the building to shape the land itself. At Igualada Cemetery (see p 32), in contrast with the man-made incision into the earth, the principal frame elements are randomly placed trees. While Igualada is dominantly stereotomic and in the ground, other schemes like the pergolas of Parets del Vallès (1985–86), Reus Rambla (1988–93) and the Avenida Icaria (1990–92) read strongly as frameworks perceived against the backdrop of the sky. In these projects, the stereotomic mass is the ground of the city into which such voids as squares and avenues are carved. Within these voids, Miralles inserted tree-like, steel-and-wood-framed shading structures, metaphors of nature in architecture. In the Civic Centre of Hostalets (1986–92) and the archery buildings for the Olympic Games (see p 38), earthwork and framework are brought together, with the frame having a real sense of emerging from, or being liberated by, the ground.

The carved and the constructed spaces of Miralles's work reveal a preoccupation with movement and a dynamic sense of restlessness, rather than a static, Newtonian conception of force. Cecil Balmond of Ove Arup & Partners explains, 'Now we see force differently, as a minimum path through a field of potential. . . . The connectivity is improvising; the equilibrium put together in ad hoc instants. The informal acts as an agent of release and architecture is free from the traditional notions of fixed grid and locked in cage – the topography of such buildings is different. . . . In the sharp juxtaposition of equilibrium there is shock, a polarising excitement of safety and risk; of uncertainty and unpredictability.'[1] In this arena, Miralles was equally adept in the realms of earthwork and framework. Retaining walls cant dramatically, creating an illusion of instability. The state of precarious balance is apparent in recurring details in the frame, where loads are eccentrically transferred from side-to-side and spanning members, instead of being simply supported, are asymmetrically propped up at one end and suspended at the other.

This idea of structure, in which nothing is at rest and subtle adjustments of action and reaction are registered, is most noticeable in the training centre at Alicante (see p 42), completed in 1993. The terms gymnastics and eurhythmics – the art of rhythmic movement – might be used to describe the conceptual underpinning of the scheme as much as its programme. Developed as a series of structures in equilibrium like the human body in motion, the circulation, the 'dancing' columns in the training hall and the undulating roof trusses are highly animated. Structures jostle one another creating interpenetrating geometries, which reveal the voyeuristic possibilities of the architectural promenade and the movement of real bodies in space.

Focusing on the physicalities of process and product, Miralles regarded the acts of drawing and construction as inseparable. For Miralles, in a manner that recalls the working method of the Italian modernist Carlo Scarpa, the building up of layers of drawn information translates directly into layered construction so that drawing and built artifact become a synonymous record of an episodic and aggregative mental process. In contrast with the pervasive culture of fast-track construction, this accumulative character is indeed genuine, for many of Miralles's buildings – like most of

Scarpa's projects – have been carried out over quite long periods of time. However, while Scarpa fetishizes craft, Miralles seeks to magnify the disjunctions and imperfections of the real. It would be difficult to imagine an aesthetic more distinct from the refinement of Scarpa's Brion Family Cemetery (near Treviso, Italy, 1969–78) than the rusted rebar, crushed rock and wild ground of Igualada Cemetery. Miralles's recent commission for an extension to the Instituto Universitario di Architettura di Venezia – where Scarpa served as dean under the motto of *Verum Ipsum Factum*, or 'Truth Through Making'[2] – would have brought the two sensibilities face to face, but now sadly will not be realized under Miralles's own hand.

Miralles professed not to be concerned with representation but – in the way that abstract impressionism values the impasto of paint on canvas over imagery – only with the blunt physical presence of construction. He noted, 'I always try to make the relationships physical: you have to be able to see through, to reach, to touch . . . I am not interested at all in allusive reality, where connections are made backwards in time, towards history, or forwards, towards a utopia; or towards a given paradigm or language . . . What interests me is a sort of incorporation.'[3] To this end, meticulous care is taken in the drawings to identify materials, components and details, and the power of the built work is indeed derived in large measure from the direct corporeal impact of overlaid textures, patterns and rhythms animated by light. Notwithstanding this preoccupation with the facts of construction, it is clear that there is also a suggestive dimension that transforms the prosaic vocabulary of building into a highly evocative language. So while Igualada Cemetery, for example, eschews literal icons, the imagination is provoked by the descent into the valley of death and the ascension; the congregation of living trees among the dead; and the pathos of the supple, almost human profile of the section.

Although there is a certain affinity in Miralles's work with the animated formal expression and tactile material aesthetic of Antoni Gaudí (1852–1926) and his contemporaries, there is also a fundamental difference. While Catalan modernisme turns away from technology and industry, placing greater moral value upon natural form, Miralles uses the products and processes of industrialized mass production as the source of his tectonic vocabulary. These industrial systems provide the ideal medium for the exploration of repetition and variation, enabling Miralles to pinpoint the exact physical conditions of each location and junction. The 'standard' section is inflected with slight variations so that extensive series of drawings are required to convey the space of even a modest building. The building section, like structure, is not static but ever-changing.

Modularity, a fundamental aspect of industrialized mass production, is exploited for its constancy and its potential for variation. The standard module, like a kind of graph paper, registers topographic variations, both in the land itself and in the fluid, subtly inflected forms of the buildings. In more recent projects, such as the training centre at Alicante, the different modularities of concrete formwork, glazed curtain wall, glass block, corrugated metal and perforated brick are juxtaposed to create a complex order of many layers. As the body moves through the spaces, the moiré effect reinforces one's experience of the building as an assembly of overlapping fragments – what Miralles might have described as a series of glances to the left and right – rather than composed views.

Having contributed so much to the Catalan renaissance, it seems fitting that Miralles was awarded the commission for the new Scottish Parliament (see p 46), a project that pivots upon the articulation of national identity. The design, described by Miralles as 'a carving in the land which reflects the act of people coming together', equates the physical body in space with the idea of the body politic. It is an exploration of the precarious balance of structure and of the fusion of building and landscape, earthwork and framework. Repetition and variation are used to generate a non-hierarchical democratic order. The scheme becomes a sedimentary record of the deposits of site, programme and culture, resulting in a collection of buildings that have distinct characters, rather than an idealized or centralized seat of power.

The parliament scheme is faithful to the themes and processes of Miralles's work, where buildings are not preconceived but coalesce through the aggregation of layer upon layer of material. Generative order is not random, but is complex and becomes precise through the reiterative processes of drawing and construction. Tectonic detail is an instrument for the registration of this precision: the cant of a column in a particular location, the juxtaposition of textures and the order of the module all play a critical role in this architecture in which physical, cultural and social landscapes negotiate a mutual terrain.

Notes
1 Cecil Balmond. 'New Structure and the Informal', *Architectural Design* (September–October 1997) pp. 88–90.
2 Kenneth Frampton. *Studies in Tectonic Culture* (Cambridge, Massachusetts and London, England: The MIT Press, 1995) p 307, where the motto *Verum Ipsum Factum* is attributed to the eighteenth-century Italian philosopher Giambattista Vico who put forward an anti-Cartesian idea of corporeal imagination.
3 Alejandro Zaera. 'A Conversation with Enric Miralles', *El Croquis*, (no 72, part 2, June 1995) p 21.

Igualada Cemetery
Igualada, Spain, 1985–96

3.1

The cemetery is an exploration of the potential of excavated ground. The only built elements that do not retain the earth are the façade and the serpentine interior wall of the services building; their free-standing status and thin planar character are emphasized by the skylight that isolates them from the buried spaces behind. In the entrance porch, a thin layer of 'ground', articulated as a filigreed screen of concrete, is peeled down to admit daylight. The cool, dark chapel is carved out of the earth and penetrated by only a few shafts of light. Its excavated section and deeply bowed concrete beams express the weight of the earth above.

Passing a gate of iron crosses, a path descends into a man-made valley that is cut into the earth. The section of the cut is asymmetrical, with two tiers of niches to the north and a single tier to the south blending imperceptibly into the existing topography. The pressure of the earth is reflected in the ever-changing character of the section, where walls of burial niches with deep arching cornices dramatically compress and release space. While the niche module remains constant, it does adjust to step down the contours and to conform to different angles of the slope. Variation within this infrastructure is provided by individualized stone plaques and urns.

As the path descends, the surrounding industrial context recedes and the space becomes inwardly focused. In contrast with the smooth concrete and orderly modular repetition of the burial niches, the ground plane is rough cast with exposed aggregate and heavy timber sleepers embedded in the concrete. At the base of the slope, the space opens into an amphitheatre of gabion retaining walls marked by randomly scattered mausolea and tombs.

Archery Ranges
Barcelona, 1989–92

3.12

Built for the 1992 Olympics and located in the Barcelona suburb of Vall d'Hebron, the archery training and competition facilities are sited between a railway embankment to the north and open ground overlooking the city to the south. The concrete roof panels of the training building emerge out of the earth and are supported by raking concrete columns. The panels overhang the gabion retaining structure to create shaded porches along the edge of the archery ranges, while a retaining wall folds deeply back into the earth to enclose group changing rooms and training facilities. Projecting concrete roofs, supported on A-frame steel columns, are connected by giant folded zinc scuppers, which are extensions of the contours of the land. Canted and tied steel columns, like archer and bow, move through a series of changing balances to respond to each particular junction. Curvilinear curtain walls act as a gridded datum plane, against which the turbulence of the roof planes and the slight variation in the angle and orientation of the steel columns are measured.

In the competition building, the repeated modules of the individual shower and changing cubicles are not rigidly ordered but, like vertebrae, adjust to conform to the contour of the escarpment. The section of the precast concrete wall – isolated from the buried portion of the building by a strip of glazing – is fluid. While the profile of the wall and the pattern of apertures on its surface remain constant, the vertical pitch and orientation of the panels shift. Externally, earth mounds cover the roof and merge with the curved head of the wall to define an elevated ground for spectators to overlook the archery ranges and the city beyond. A steel canopy, free of the exigencies of the earth, is rational and linear.

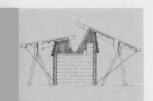

3.13

National Training Centre for Rhythmic Gymnastics, Alicante, Spain, 1989–93

The building comprises a series of overlapping, interwoven topographies, in which the stereotomic vocabulary of excavation and retaining walls plays a subordinate role to the dominant language of elevated highway interchanges and bridges. The planes of reference are provided by the flat slab of the performance and training floor and by the underbelly of the roof. Between these built abstractions of earth and sky, interior topography is created by spectator circulation, observation galleries and seating.

The primary public entrance defines the long north façade and a series of switchback ramps – concrete in the open air, a steel-framed tunnel inside – delivers spectators to an elevated circulation spine between the training hall and the competition arena. Seating is asymmetrically dispersed around the competition floor and the corners of the arena are fractured, providing glimpses into adjacent spaces and out to the external world. In the training hall, work-out areas are randomly distributed and changing rooms for the athletes are tucked under the spectator stands between the competition and training areas.

The steel roof structure delineates an exterior topography that echoes the surrounding mountains. Longitudinal steel box trusses are irregularly shaped in direct response to structural forces. The two outer trusses bear on a series of massive concrete piers; the central truss spans the competition area and is supported on clusters of raked tubular-steel columns in the training hall. Beyond the limit of the trusses, masts and suspension cables carry the overhanging roof above the entrance ramps. Just as the roof structure has a hybrid character, the enclosing wall of the building is a montage of overlapped modular systems.

Scottish Parliament
Edinburgh, 1997–2002

3.14 The parliament is a collection of new and existing buildings designed to respond to the immediate urban setting and to the larger context of the dramatic landscape surrounding Edinburgh. To emphasize the non-hierarchical and aggregative nature of the scheme, the leaflike form of the debating chamber is not unique but one of a series of similar volumes. Although early plans for the inwardly focused chamber were bilaterally symmetrical about a cross axis, subtle asymmetries are now being introduced in the seating plan and the enclosure of the space. The apparently thick east wall is a double structure sculpted by the visitors' gallery and by voids that bring light into the public foyer below. The west wall is envisaged as a thinner translucent assembly in which a few apertures frame key views of iconic monuments and landscapes. The studied equilibrium of the chamber's timber-trussed roof structure, which is both supported and suspended, is an apt reminder of the balance of interests needed to forge a nation.

The private offices of MPs are located along the west boundary of the site, distanced from the other buildings by a private cloistered garden at first-floor level. Expressed as a series of repeated modules that democratically provide equal space and amenity for all, they do not conform to a rigid grid, but slip to a softer contour. The detailing of the bay windows varies slightly from office to office to create a 'façade of individuals'. The complex's parking and vehicular services are tucked under the garden, which extends to the south, fusing imperceptibly with the natural landscape. This topography is internalized in the longitudinal vaults that define the public entrance foyer.

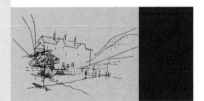

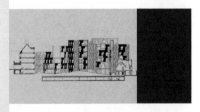

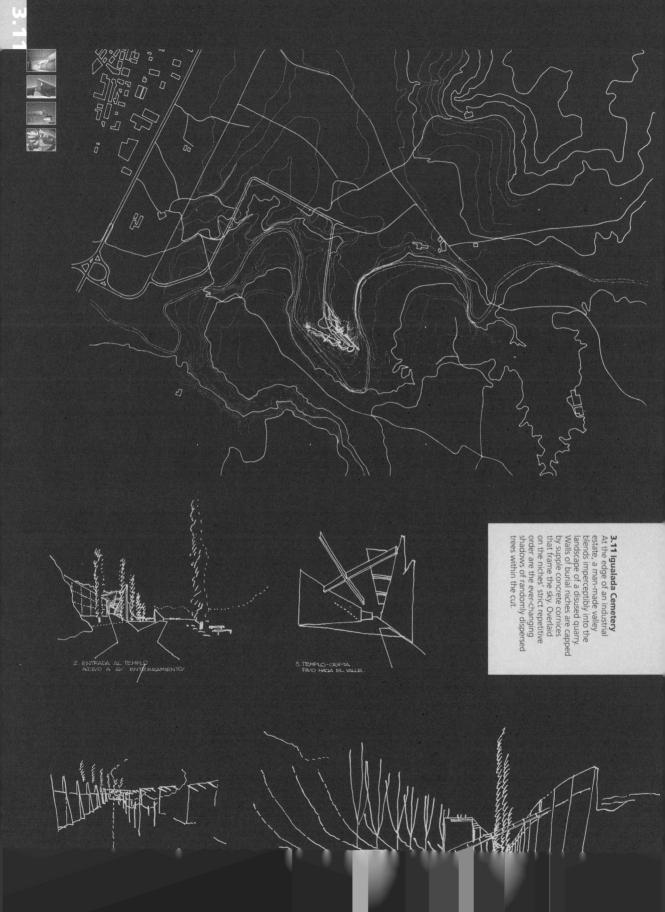

2. ENTRADA AL TEMPLO
ACCESO A LOS ENTERRAMIENTOS.

3. TEMPLO-CRIPTA
PASO HACIA EL VALLE.

3.11 Igualada Cemetery
At the edge of an industrial
estate, a man-made valley
blends imperceptibly into the
landscape of a disused quarry.
Walls of burial niches are capped
by supple concrete cornices
that frame the sky. Overlaid
on the niches' strict repetitive
order are the ever-changing
shadows of randomly dispersed
trees within the cut.

Family Tombs

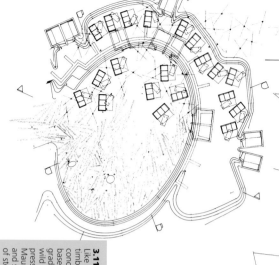

Section details of burial niches

3.11 Igualada Cemetery
Like logs washed downstream, timber sleepers embedded in the concrete ground congregate at the base of the cut. Rusty gabions – gradually being overgrown with wild vegetation – bulge with the pressure of the earth behind. Mausolea are carved into the earth and screened from view by 'veils' of steel and translucent glass.

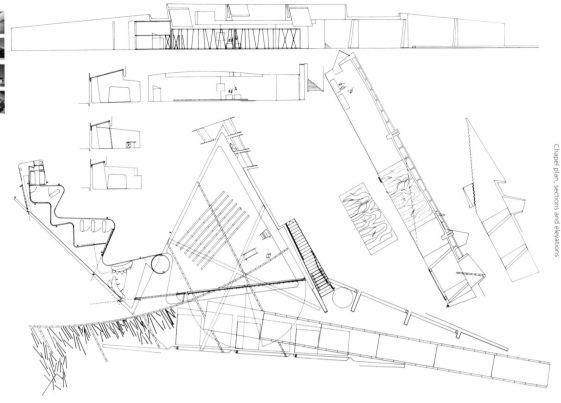

Chapel plan, sections and elevations

3.11 Igualada Cemetery
The free-standing wall of the services building, made from layered and interlocking concrete panels, is a planar version of the more complex three-dimensional panels that form the burial niches. Within, a tall toplit circulation space leads to the morgue and sacristy, which are screened behind a serpentine wall.

3.12 Archery Ranges
The structure of the training building is dynamic rather than static, reflecting both the undulating topography from which the building emerges and the athletic activity that it houses. The gabion retaining wall folds back to provide group changing and training rooms – a social landscape, augmented by the warmth of wood, red-oxide-painted steel, brick and terracotta.

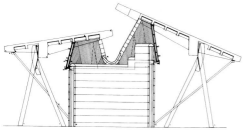

Cross sections

Long section

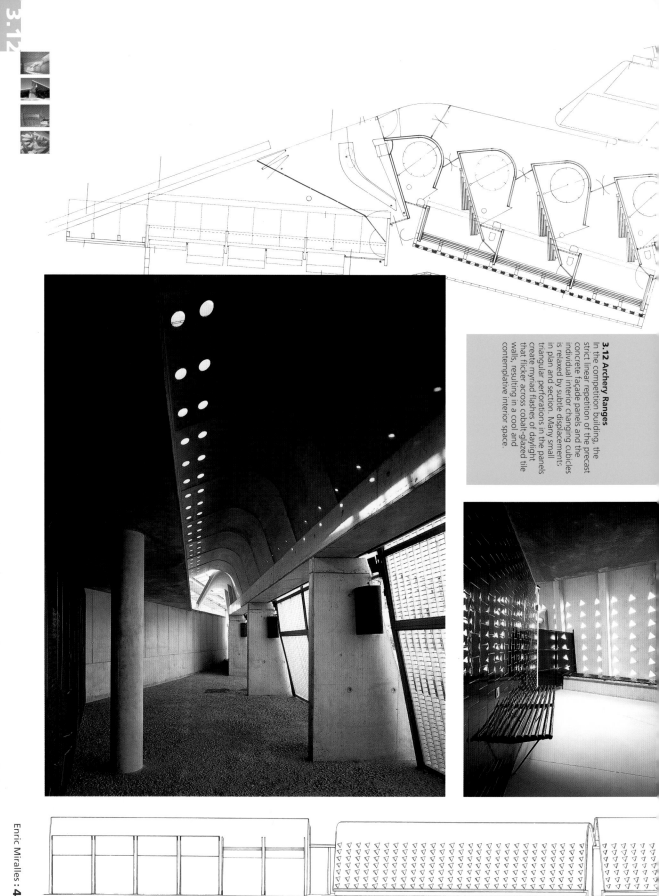

3.12 Archery Ranges
In the competition building, the strict linear repetition of the precast concrete façade panels and the individual interior changing cubicles is relaxed by subtle displacements in plan and section. Many small triangular perforations in the panels create myriad flashes of daylight that flicker across cobalt-glazed tile walls, resulting in a cool and contemplative interior space.

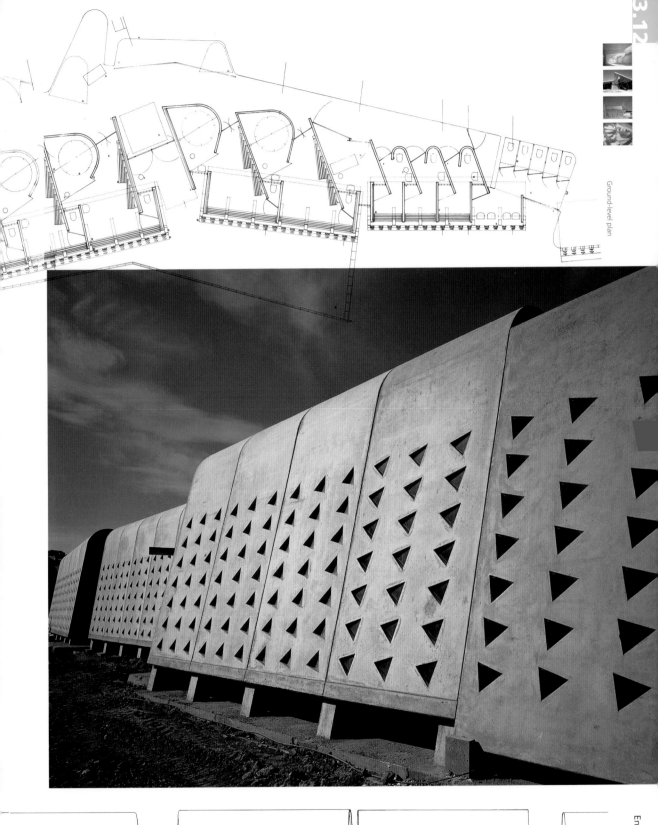

Long section

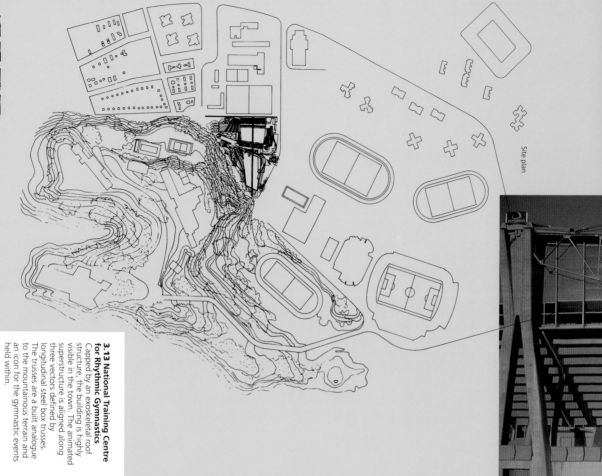

Site plan

3.13 National Training Centre for Rhythmic Gymnastics

Capped by an exoskeletal roof structure, the building is highly visible in the town. The animated superstructure is aligned along three vectors defined by longitudinal steel box trusses. The trusses are a built analogue to the mountainous terrain and an icon for the gymnastic events held within.

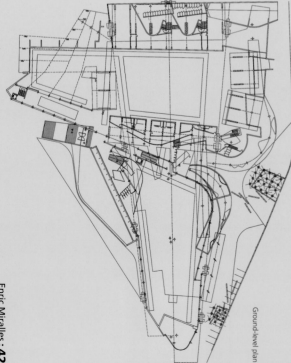

Ground-level plan

Twelfth-level plan

Roof plan and sections

A   A'

B   B'

C   C'

D   D'

E   E'

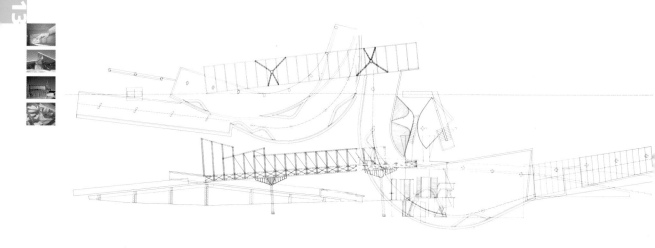

3.13 National Training Centre for Rhythmic Gymnastics
A sense of precarious balance is expressed by clusters of dancing columns in the training area. Ramps wrap around the building externally and penetrate through interior spaces; with both the public and the athletes in motion and on view, the distinction between spectator and performer is blurred.

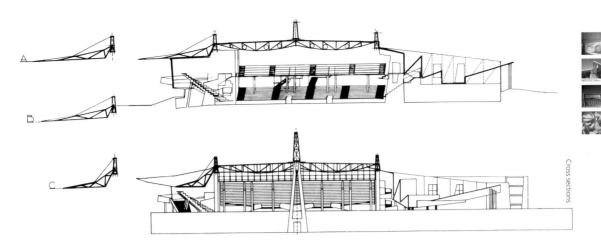

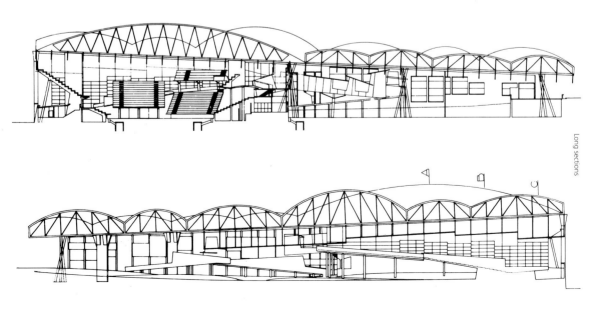

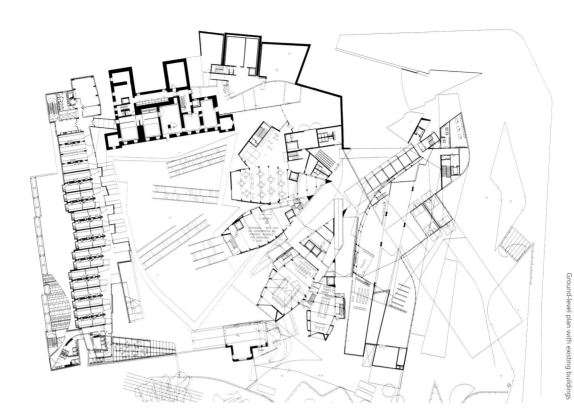

Elevation

Elevation

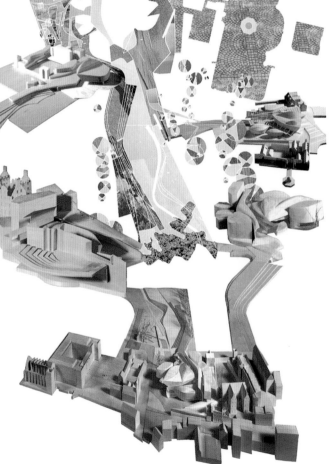

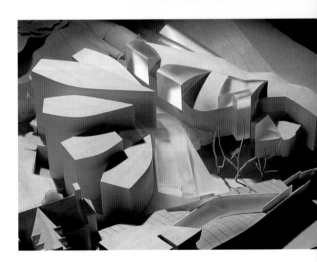

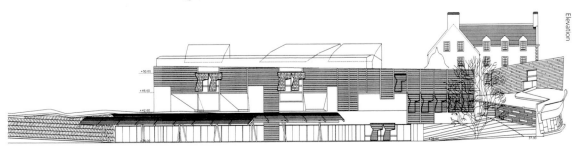

Elevation

Enric Miralles : **47**

3.21

3.22

3.23

3.24

Günter Behnisch

Situationsarchitektur

3.20

The work of Günter Behnisch, which reflects his belief that architecture is an image of society, has evolved radically during a career that has spanned nearly fifty years. Opening his office in Germany just after the Second World War, Behnisch – like many architects of the time – enthusiastically embraced industrialized, prefabricated systems of construction as the means to quickly and economically rebuild his country. Educational institutions of all kinds, a top priority during the reconstruction effort and as the postwar economy of Germany expanded, have accounted for the vast majority of his commissions. Indicative of the direction of a number of his early projects, the building for the Technical University of Ulm, completed in 1963, used precast concrete structure and cladding to construct the largest completely prefabricated public building in Germany at that time.

However, while systems building was fast and efficient, Behnisch increasingly found it to be limiting, and with the design for the buildings and grounds of the 1972 Olympic Games in Munich, his work took a new direction. Although the canopy over the Olympic stadium made use of advanced, highly industrialized systems of construction, each detail was custom-designed and technology was suddenly made subservient to the hand. In addition, a new synergy between building and site emerged. The waste ground of a former rubbish tip was reclaimed and heavily recontoured to create a 'natural' amphitheatre for the stadium, and the formal language of the canopy was designed as an extension of the landscape. This new ground – which provided views of the events for non-paying spectators that were as good as those inside the stadium – was also conceived as a social landscape aimed at democratizing the spectacle of the Olympic Games.

Behnisch's subsequent work has focused on the development of a more humane form of modernism, characterized by spatial, material and tectonic differentiation. Systems building has been supplanted by *Situationsarchitektur*, where each detail of the building arises out of unique conditions of place and need. The topography of this architecture is the culturally specific political landscape of Germany.

Shaping a new image for the country in the wake of totalitarianism, Behnisch equates a diversity of tectonic detail with individuality, pluralism, freedom and democracy. Central to this approach is the premise that no single order is allowed to define the whole. In lieu of a unifying grid or a clear hierarchy of parts, Behnisch states, 'Life requires order of another kind. We think more like nature. There is order, but it is individualised and – like the debris after a flood – open-ended and unpredictable. It is more hopeful.'[1] This principle is played out in a number of ways. Within each building, many ordering systems are juxtaposed but are not harmoniously resolved. Standard modules for repetitive programmatic elements, such as classrooms, labs or offices are eschewed, with rooms either being uniquely configured or having the potential to become unique through components that can be manipulated by individual occupants. In a similar manner, multiple structural grids come together in generous central circulation spaces – volumes of Piranesian complexity typically defined by glazed enclosures and occupied by combinations of stairs, ramps and stepped ramps. The enclosures act as social condensers, using transparency, movement and visual complexity to foster openness and unprescribed social interaction.

The tectonic language of the building envelope is also highly differentiated, not by custom-made systems as in the Olympic stadium, but by the unconventional combination of standard systems in overlapping layers, each with its own geometry and orientation. Instead of the systems-built façade, which might be characterized as being merely the sum of its repetitive parts, recent buildings, like the Albert Schweitzer School at Bad Rappenau (see p 56), are indicative of an approach that exploits the inherent multilayered nature of contemporary construction to create complexity. Primary structure, curtain wall and shading systems are overlaid to generate an unresolved and unanticipated whole. Each junction is designed with reference to its unique place and role in the building. Stairs and balustrades – differentiated from stairway to stairway, floor to floor, and even side to side of a single flight – become a particular focus of Behnisch's tectonic invention.

Order is further undermined by the use of colour, which does not conform to either the profile or the module of the components to which it is applied, but instead highlights fragments and skips from bay to bay in accordance with an intuitive, non-rational logic. In tandem with colour, mirrors interfere with the integrity of planar surfaces and building components, a device that Behnisch suggests is inspired by the Baroque churches of southern Germany, extraordinary spatial apparitions that seemingly liberate structure from bearing weight and blur the distinction between nature and architecture.

While this tectonic language – almost playful in its rejection of total order in favour of the development of individualized orders – is eminently well-suited to the design of such environments as schools, Behnisch uses the same vocabulary in all manner of more typically staid institutional buildings. Indeed, the notion of play is taken quite seriously: believing that man is free only when at play, Behnisch operates on the premise that 'the disorder of the dance' is ultimately more important than order. In the Plenary Complex for the German Bundestag in Bonn (see p 60) – the most serious of buildings – the subversion of a single total order by using many incomplete and conflicting organizational systems becomes overtly political and shows Behnisch's desire to reflect in built form a multifaceted, tolerant cultural identity for Germany. The Bundestag, in fact, is the single project that most clearly crystallizes the principles underlying Behnisch's work.

The Bonn complex is a loose confederation of orthogonal pavilions, each adjusting in a relaxed way to local conditions and connections to existing buildings. Without unifying axes, a non-hierarchical whole is characterized by a freedom of parts. In this organization, two contrasting threads of influence can be discerned: the orderly form-giving hand of Mies van der Rohe and the non-rational, form-finding hand of Hans Scharoun. There is a subtle play between a rational sense of order and the intuitive episode, which is also present in Behnisch's earlier Hysolar Institute (Stuttgart, 1987) and the Post and Communications Museum (Frankfurt, 1990).

The circular form of the plenary hall is inflected on the upper level by visitor galleries and enclosing walls laid out on an orthogonal grid. In marked contrast to the Berlin Reichstag, there is no centralizing dome over the chamber but instead a neutrally gridded glazed ceiling, and even the regularity of this element is disrupted by the ad hoc insertion of mirrors. Ultimately, the idealized circle is only realized when the Members of Parliament are in their seats. Likewise, although the President's office and conference rooms are placed hierarchically facing the Rhine, the suspended stairway that connects these rooms to the Plenary Hall floats freely in the plan and is wrapped in a nest of random wood battens that clearly contrasts the non-rational with the rational. Because of the juxtaposition of many systems, the order of the building cannot be understood a priori but is only appreciated through the direct experience of the body in space.

The Bundestag's transparency – the fully glazed enclosure around the Plenary Hall and the external envelope – establishes a strong visual connection with nature and pays homage to the architect Hans Schwippert who designed the first glazed legislative chamber in Bonn in 1949 as a symbol of the importance of openness in the workings of governments. The layering of the façades and their capacity to be manipulated by the occupants permit an ever-changing visage quite unconcerned with static monumentality. A lack of pretension is also evident in the modest material character of the building. This project is an astonishing political statement, rendered more poignant by the reunification of Germany and the decision, taken before construction was even complete, to abandon Bonn as capital.

Behnisch's avoidance of monumentality and his belief in highly differentiated detail have long prevented him from undertaking commissions for the very large buildings that comprise the work of many contemporary practices. However, now that Germany's small-scale, localized architectural infrastructure is highly developed, the office has inevitably had to take on such sizeable projects at home and abroad as the State Insurance Building in Lübeck (see p 66) and the Harbourside Centre for the Performing Arts in Bristol, England (see p 70). Regardless of scale, the principles of a loosely organized field of parts that does not coalesce into an easily identifiable whole, the play between the rational and intuitive, and the subversive detail remain the touchstones of a tectonic language that – rooted in the politics of pluralist democracy – is complex, diverse and many layered. Yet, Behnisch's buildings do not require an overt political forum. Their value, which is relevant globally as well as locally, is in the provision of stimulating, differentiated environments in which ordinary people live, work and learn. Their message is an enduring commitment to the social contract of architecture.

Note
1 Author's conversation with Günter Behnisch, 18 May 1999.

Albert Schweitzer School
Bad Rappenau, Germany, 1987–91

3.21

Designed for children with learning difficulties, the school provides an environment that instills a sense of pride among its occupants. A generous two-storey glazed central hall with an open stairway forms the spatial and social centre of the building. The slender cross section of the hall ensures a close relationship with the outside world, and the fractured massing and sloping roof planes, in addition to lending the building a domestic character, are tightly integrated into the contours of the site. Each classroom is individually shaped in plan, section and elevation, and the tectonic detail is highly differentiated. The in-situ concrete columns of the classroom wings are distinguished from the raking steel prop in the central hall. The visual integrity and structural logic of the concrete columns are blurred by blue stain, clearly delineated at the base and feathered out at the top. The detailing of the stair and balcony balustrades varies to respond to particular locations; the handrail does not obediently level off at the landing but continues its upward trajectory, while a second, lower rail performs the duty required by the building regulations.

On a different module from the concrete and steel primary structures, castellated steel I-sections brace the curtain wall of the central hall, which is overlaid by an independently ordered system of sun blinds in brightly coloured stripes and solids. The blinds are programmed to respond to changing light conditions during the day and are also manually operable. The rich range of spaces, materials and details creates an atmosphere that is playful and congenial and, by taking the needs of children seriously, offers a stimulating setting for learning and development.

Plenary Complex for the German Bundestag
Bonn, 1982–92

3.22 Tucked among the trees, this modest seat of the German federal government is designed as a series of pavilions dispersed informally on natural terraces stepping down to the Rhine. Movement through the buildings, which is neither central nor axial, reinforces the non-hierarchical character of the scheme. An entrance foyer, shared by Members of Parliament and visitors, forms the east side of a small square adjacent to the street on the upper terrace. A grand stairway is positioned obliquely to carry MPs from the entrance down to the Plenary Hall, and a VIP entrance by the river is likewise skewed and off-centre. On the lowest terrace, a restaurant links the new complex and the existing buildings to the north, while a pavilion to the south houses offices for the Bundestag vice presidents, the Chancellor and the staff.

In the foyer, the order established by the regular structural grid and reinforced by the galvanized metal-mesh ceiling is confounded by loosely dispersed fluorescent lights, shards of coloured glass and a line of yellow neon that directs the eye down to the Plenary Hall. To ease the flow of space at the foot of the grand stairway, a single column in the grid is omitted and its load transferred by an expressed beam. The pitch and yaw of the balustrades, with timber and glass aligned differently, establish their independence from the orthogonal; the glass floats at the base of the stairway and slices into the concrete as it ascends. Externally, balcony, balustrade and sunshade details change from floor to floor, defying an all-embracing order.

State Insurance Building, Schleswig-Holstein
Lübeck, Germany, 1992–97

3.23 Located at the edge of the city and alongside a landscape of allotment gardens, this scheme provides offices for 1,100 civil servants who manage state benefits for the citizens of Schleswig-Holstein. The building is enormous compared to the Albert Schweitzer School, but its organizational principles are the same. Wings of offices radiate from a central hall that holds the entrance, vertical circulation and the major communal spaces of the building, including a staff restaurant and training classrooms. The star-shaped form ensures that, from the exterior, the full scale of the 398,490-square-feet (37,000-square-metre) building cannot be seen from any single vantage point. The shallow cross sections of the central hall and the offices allow an intimate relationship with the outside world. Landscape penetrates to the heart of the building between the office wings, and shared conference facilities on the top level look out over a planted roof.

The potentially relentless character of the office grid is eroded by voids and social spaces, which bring light and communal life to the building. The structural grids of the radiating wings come together in the central hall where geometric complexity is augmented by colour, mirrors and the reflective properties of the glass. The repetitive and systematic module of the office cladding reads strongly externally, but it is mitigated by adjustable louvred sunshades and by variously coloured spandrel panels that follow an independent logic. The finish of selected panels is iridescent so that the colours change subtly in different light conditions.

Harbourside Centre for the Performing Arts
Bristol, England, 1996–98

Although the formal language of the performing arts centre is very different from the Bundestag, the concept of a loose federation of parts remains constant. The many geometries that converge on the site are ideally suited to Behnisch's pluralist sensibilities and ensure that each element of the programme can have its own formal and tectonic logic. The scheme includes a two-thousand-seat concert hall, a five-hundred-seat hall for dance and ballet, public foyers, a rehearsal hall, dressing rooms and offices. Public cafés, restaurants and shops are provided at ground level.

In the large auditorium, which is aligned diagonally with an existing square, the audience is wrapped around the performers in irregular tiers of seats. The small hall, which abuts an existing dock building to the north, is built in a more conventional shoebox format, placed perpendicular to the water's edge. The northernmost wing of the centre, which houses the stage door and retail at ground level, with the rehearsal room and offices above, completes the east side of the square. Between the auditoria, the foyers form the heart of the interior public space, with the primary entrance from the square and a secondary entrance from a public path along the harbour. A complex array of stairs leads up to the stalls foyer on the first floor, and on to upper foyers that serve the balcony seats.

The exploitation of changing qualities of light has figured strongly in shaping the scheme. The non-orthogonal geometry of the folded skin of metal and glass is designed to give the city a shimmering landmark animated by sun, clouds and reflections from the water.

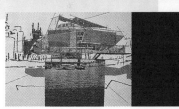

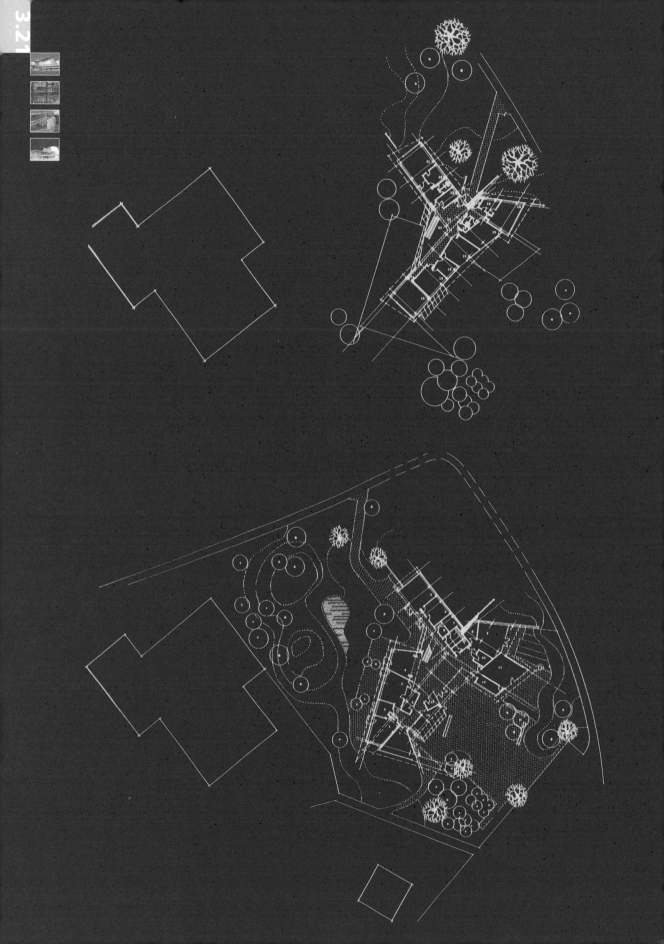

3.21 Albert Schweitzer School
Located at the edge of a residential area in a small town, the building is tucked into its sloping site, making both floors accessible at ground level. An entrance marked by a concrete chimney leads into the upper level of a double-height glazed central hall flanked by administration offices and classrooms.

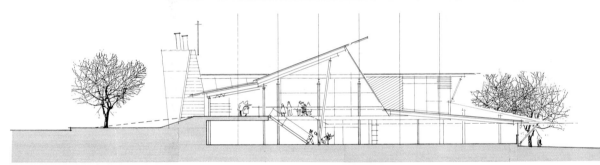

Long section

3.21 Albert Schweitzer School
A generous stairway connects to the lower level, where rooms for art, music and cooking open directly onto outdoor play areas. The multiple ordering systems employed by Behnisch are reflected in the fractured massing of the building and in the layered façades. Several structural systems are brought together in the central hall, where they coexist but do not resolve into a single overriding order. This rich mix of materials and details is as playful as the children who inhabit the building.

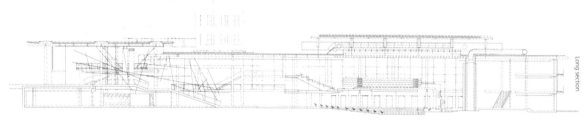

Long section

3.22 Plenary Complex for the German Bundestag
This central seat for the German government was designed as a loosely ordered collection of pavilions that adapts to the sloping terrain and to the adjoining buildings. The detailing of balconies and shading devices varies from place to place so that the public face of the building is always changing.

3.22 Plenary Complex for the German Bundestag
MPs and members of the public use the same entrance from the upper terrace. The gridded order of the entrance foyer is counteracted by coloured glass, mirrors and neon lights that float freely in the space. The stairway that carries MPs down to the chamber is grand in scale but informal in character.

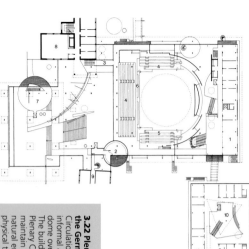

3.22 Plenary Complex for the German Bundestag

Circulation through the building is informal and there is no centralizing dome over the Plenary Chamber. The building's glass façades and the Plenary Chamber's glazed enclosure maintain a close rapport with the natural environment and their physical transparency suggests the openness of the democratic political process. A stairway wrapped in a 'bird's nest' is a reminder of the importance of non-rational beauty as an antidote to pure reason.

Upper-level plan

Lower-level plan

Schnitt **cc** M 1:1000

Site plan

3.23 State Insurance Building

Although large in scale, the building maintains an intimate relationship with nature. Between the slender radiating fingers of offices, each landscape is developed to have a particular and identifiable character. The superimposed orders of curtain wall, adjustable sunscreens and multicoloured spandrel panels break down the scale of the building and animate its façades.

3.23 State Insurance Building
The many structural orders of the building jostle one another in the central circulation and social space. Geometric complexity is amplified by colour that, rather than obeying a logical order, is used intuitively. Mirrors, reflections in the glass and the changing patterns of light and shadow generate an architectural vitality intended to stimulate spontaneous, unstructured social interaction.

Günter Behnisch : **68**

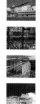

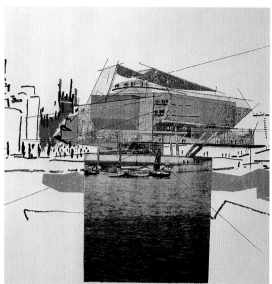

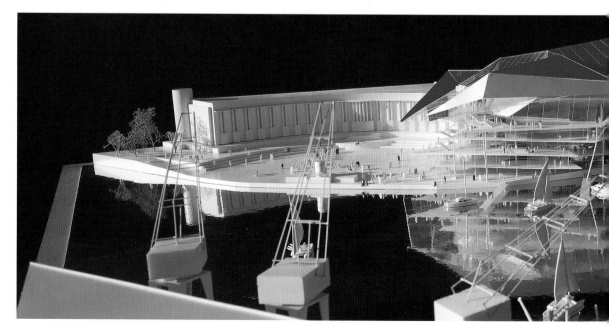

3.24 Harbourside Centre for the Performing Arts

The form of the building is distilled from the many geometries already present on the site. A central space separates the two performance halls and provides a public connection between a city square to the north and a footpath along the water's edge. The glazed façades, animated by people in the foyers and on the stairs wrapping the auditoria, become emblematic of the social role of this public building in the city.

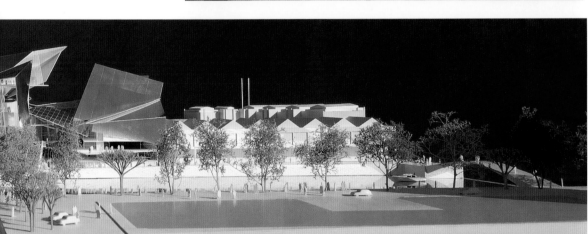

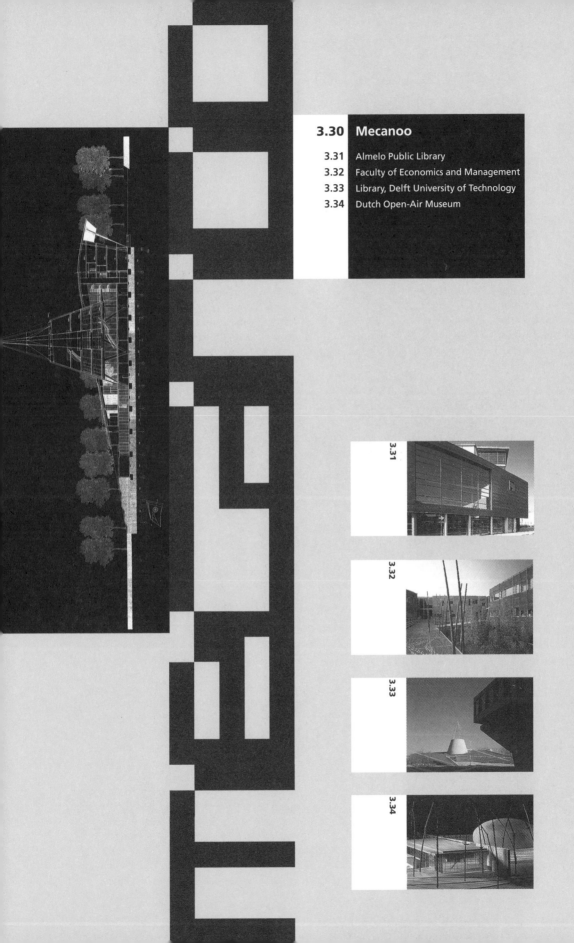

3.30 Mecanoo

3.31

3.32

3.33

3.34

Mecanoo
Revising the Ideal

When the scheme submitted by a group of architecture students was declared winner of the 1982 competition to design new housing on Rotterdam's Kruisplein, Mecanoo moved directly from education into practice. The Kruisplein project, built while they were still students, prolonged their architectural training by several years and was a highly unorthodox apprenticeship, characterized by forays onto construction sites to glean information to detail their own building. This spirited, even playful sense of adventure – symbolized by a logo of a diver leaping into the unknown and a name derived from a well-known construction toy – has endured as the work of the office has matured. Faithful to the manner in which they began, the architects have continued to search out and test ideas, not through ideology or theory, but through the pragmatic reality of construction.

The Kruisplein project emerged at a time when the heady ideological debates of CIAM (Congrès Internationaux d'Architecture Moderne) and Team Ten – both with strong Dutch constituencies – had lost impetus and when the professions were reeling from the student upheavals of 1968. In response to the disillusionment with modernism and the crisis of professional confidence, architectural education had embraced the social sciences, turning away from formal and aesthetic issues as determinants in the making of the built artifact. Mecanoo's scheme for Kruisplein, with its careful integration of social responsibility with aesthetic concerns, launched an assault aimed at restoring architecture as a design discipline – a campaign that has invigorated the current generation of young Dutch architects, propelling many to positions of international prominence. Mecanoo, however, stands out because it operates under a collective rubric rather than projecting the signature style of individual partners.

The socio-political and geographic context of the Netherlands has been a critical factor in shaping Mecanoo's collective working method and the practice's buildings. The strong commitment to social democracy – the surrendering of individual interests to achieve common goals – is deeply rooted in the history of a nation that has been literally dredged up from the sea and where survival has depended upon a communal responsibility for keeping the water out. Because land is scarce, it is densely occupied and its use is highly prescribed. It is not surprising, therefore, that the work of Dutch architects, including Mecanoo, increasingly blurs the distinction between architecture, planning, urban design, landscape and infrastructure.

Inheriting the ideology that architecture shapes and reflects the matrix of human society, as espoused by Dutch architect and urban planner Hendrik Berlage, Mecanoo has built its reputation on a working method that springs from the critical transformation of typology. This method, which grew out of the strong analytical design emphasis in the architects' training at Delft in the early 1980s, was described contemporaneously in the influential writings of Donald Schön, which set out a new socially engaged mode of professional operation. In what Schön terms as a 'conversation with the situation', the ideal type is altered in response to the specific conditions of each project and the changing patterns and configurations of human life. Mecanoo notes, 'The problem is constantly revised, reshaped and reframed . . . As professionals, therefore, rather than protecting the status quo, we become agents of change . . . reformulating the problem, not merely solving it.'[1]

The brief for the Kruisplein housing for young people implicitly acknowledged that the prevalent nuclear family house was not meeting the needs of growing sectors of the urban population. Mecanoo responded by creating dwellings that allowed for varying degrees of community interaction and privacy and that, without aping the appearance of surrounding historic buildings, departed from utopian modernism by being carefully integrated into their context. This sensibility spawned numerous typological variants on an internally flexible neutral dwelling – an exploration of the *plan libre* – which became the basis for the several thousand units of public housing that Mecanoo has designed and built since Kruisplein. As commissions have become more varied, the same critical analysis has been applied to other building types. In such recent projects as Almelo Public Library (see p 80) and Rochussenstraat in Rotterdam (1991–95), which combines housing, offices, shops and social services in a single building, Mecanoo developed hybrid typologies to respond to complex amalgams of urban use. The design for the library at Delft University of Technology (see p 88) radically revises typology to absorb changing technology.

The emphasis on manipulating the abstraction of the idealized type to reflect the real is expressed in the formal and material character of the architects' buildings. A number of their housing schemes use material distinctions to clarify contextual relationships, distinguishing, for example, the hierarchy of front, back and side, or the types of tower, terrace and villa. In other projects, many different uses are brought together in single volumes with unifying façades; within these deceptively simple statements, programmatic specificity is identified by changes of material. While form does not necessarily follow function in the strict modernist sense, the formal and material heterogeneity of Mecanoo's buildings elucidates their contextual and programmatic complexity.

In addition to acting as a programmatic code, materials are employed to augment corporeal experience. At Delft library, for example, the blue wall is so intensely saturated with colour that it seems to shimmer, heightening the honorific presence of the books. Along the southern façade, the inner corridor wall of the offices – a collage of several types of transparent and translucent glass – generates a rich, changing tapestry of daylight in the central hall. In a number of projects, the opposition between rough and refined, complex and simple, new and old is exploited, resulting in surprising contrasts and a variety of atmospheres. Throughout Mecanoo's work, there is an obvious sense of pleasure in exploring the juxtaposition of materials and in creating a sensate backdrop to inhabitation.

The rich material character of Mecanoo's buildings is highly articulated in façades that are frequently layered to reconcile the conflicting demands of internal programme and external context. The cladding of the Faculty of Economics and Management at Utrecht University (see p 84), while lavish in effect, is economically achieved by a simple, regular curtain wall, which provides the weathertight enclosure. Visual and tactile richness is found in an outer layer that – liberated from the obligations of plan, section and weather – is freely configured and ambiguous in scale. Together with the courtyard landscapes, these façades do not adjust to their context, but instead – in the Italian Renaissance tradition of using the city as a setting for tragedy and nature for comedy – create their own context as a theatrical backdrop to the life of the building. Rather than amplifying a natural geography, the topographical character of Mecanoo's work is invented like the landscape of Holland itself. As an antidote to the flat terrain that is virtually featureless save for an ever-present network of man-made dykes and canals, the artifice seems singularly appropriate.

The manipulation of topography for effect becomes even more dramatic in Delft Library. Here, built form and land form are integrated into a single emphatic flourish so that the library reveals itself primarily as a landscape that establishes a new context for the adjacent building.

It is almost as if the ground has been lifted up like a carpet and the library swept discreetly underneath it. However, notwithstanding its many self-effacing qualities, the building provides a spectacular social landscape for the campus, which operates externally on the accessible planted roof and internally as revealed by a transparent skin. The visual openness of the building's programme generates a new typology far removed from the traditional image of the library as secure bastion of knowledge.

As the work of Mecanoo has matured, the tectonic language of the practice's buildings has been characterized by an increasingly sophisticated integration of building technology with the representational and expressive potential of construction. Indicative of the concerns shaping a number of current projects, the exterior envelope of the library at Delft is a triple-glazed, ventilated climate wall that, together with the planted roof, offers acoustic and temperature insulation. Gradual evaporation of rain-water held by the turf provides natural cooling in the summer, and the use of ground water to temper the interior climate minimizes mechanical servicing. The structural components, in addition to increasing the sense of drama in the interior space, work hard environmentally; each column's star-shaped foot is wrapped with perforated metal, which is a supply duct for fresh air. However, although Delft uses innovative engineering strategies, technique is intentionally understated in favour of the heightened sensory experience derived from the sheer pleasure of form, material and detail.

The work of Mecanoo is preoccupied with the reshaping of the ideal to accommodate the changing institutions that comprise the spaces of human society. The reappraisal of typology and the fusion of landscape and built form generate a tectonic language that explores representation and clearly relishes the direct physical experience of the building. For Mecanoo, there can be 'no form without restrictions . . . no architecture without knowing the luxury of its materials'.[2] In the practice's work, architecture is not simply an intellectual construct but a physical artifact that seeks to touch all the senses.

Notes

1 Mecanoo. 'The Reflective Architect' in *Mecanoo, Michigan Architecture Papers 6* (Ann Arbor: College of Architecture + Urban Planning, University of Michigan, 1999) p 17.
2 Kees Somer. 'Architecture as Celebration' in *Mecanoo* (Rotterdam: Uitgeverij 010 Publishers, 1995) p VII. Taken from Mecanoo's statement describing the practice's pavilion in the Biennale for Young Dutch Architects in 1985, published in 'Biennale jonge Nederlandse architecten', Wonen/TABK 19-20 (1985) p 27.

Almelo Public Library
Almelo, The Netherlands, 1991–94

3.31

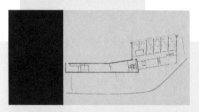

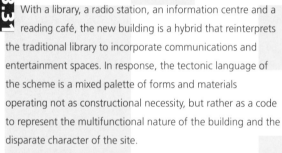

With a library, a radio station, an information centre and a reading café, the new building is a hybrid that reinterprets the traditional library to incorporate communications and entertainment spaces. In response, the tectonic language of the scheme is a mixed palette of forms and materials operating not as constructional necessity, but rather as a code to represent the multifunctional nature of the building and the disparate character of the site.

The structural system is also heterogeneous. The façade's regular grid of circular columns along a smooth arc is set against the irregular spacing and orientation of the concrete fins that define the faceted glazed wall at ground level. Internally, a row of paired columns shifts again to a second regular metre at the edge of the void. The implied lack of structural continuity is also evident in the split-level section and along the street where the circular columns at ground level fail to materialize in the large windows of the copper-clad façade above.

At the rear of the building, in the so-called fish tail, angled concrete piers and expressed beams transform into fin walls, which, in turn, define study areas. At the point where the structure becomes most dense, the visual weight of the fin walls is challenged by the fact that they hover just 11.8 inches (30 cm) above the ground, supported on slender tubular steel posts. The dialogue between weight and weightlessness continues in the spine of the building, which is a densely colonized, brick-clad earthbound solid at one end and an uninhabited toplit circulation void at the other.

Faculty of Economics and Management
Utrecht, The Netherlands, 1991–95

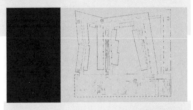

3.32

Two orders of space – large, public facilities and repetitive ranks of classrooms and offices – are laid out to form a series of quadrangles in this academic building. Within this framework, material and formal manipulations transform the typology, resulting in a building that is far from traditional. The two-storey glazed bar along the street becomes an enormous vitrine in which the public functions of the building are flamboyantly displayed. The lecture halls, seemingly weightless volumes that float half in half out of the glazed enclosure, are clad in different materials, ranging from ordinary expanded metal mesh to finely finished wood.

In other areas of the building, form and material are deployed to enhance sensory experience. The courtyards are tactile spaces, where architecture and landscape combine to create spirited open-air public rooms of great character. The Zen court, inspired by Japanese meditation gardens, is static in nature. In contrast, the water court reflects changing weather and seasons and is in a state of flux. The central jungle court is animated by the colours and leaf textures of bamboo and by patterns of human occupation. The plans of the quadrangles are distorted, a particularly effective device in the exaggerated perspective of the water court, which tapers virtually to a single viewpoint at its north end while opening to the world to the south. The preoccupation with landscape is internalized by ramped corridors of classrooms and dramatic stairways that shoot obliquely across voids to form an unexpected interior topography.

Library, Delft University of Technology
Delft, The Netherlands, 1992–97

Tucked discreetly beneath a raised lawn, the building's external modesty is an excellent foil for the interior drama of the vast reference and reading room, where a giant cone supported on splayed steel columns houses four levels of toplit study rooms. The cone pierces the green expanse of the roof, acting as a beacon on the campus, day and night. Within, the visitor is poised between the cerebral pleasure of electronically disseminated information and the sensory enjoyment of being able to touch and smell books. In honour of the written word, a dramatic four-storey tower of books that includes 80,000 of the most frequently requested volumes is silhouetted against a vibrant ultramarine wall.

Tectonic ingenuity heightens the experience of the building and creates a dialogue between weight and weightlessness. In contrast with Almelo, where structure is highly differentiated, at Delft difference is suppressed. Instead of expressing all the forces at work, the illusion is that the structure is hardly working at all. The columns range from one to four storeys in height, but due to their slender, uniform profile, their delicate connection to the roof and the concealed lighting of their heads, the roof appears to float. The glazed skin, designed as a tempered climate wall, also plays an important role in the perception of the building. Black and silver mullions overlay the regular glazing module with an irregular rhythm of horizontal dashed lines, detaching wall from roof and augmenting the illusion of weightlessness.

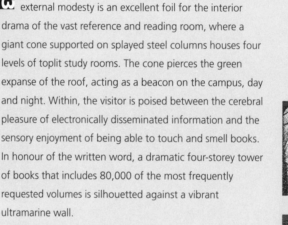

Dutch Open-Air Museum
Arnhem, The Netherlands, 1998–2000

3.34

It is ironic for the museum at Arnhem to be part of this body of work, where landscape is often artifice. The museum is primarily a landscape, a park where historic buildings from throughout the Netherlands have been transplanted. Therefore, while the site offers a genuine topography, the architecture is in some sense artificial. In supplying the museum with new indoor amenities, which are less dependent on the weather, Mecanoo has judiciously chosen to intervene at the scale of the landscape and to downplay the building. A 475.7-foot-long (145 metre) brick wall – a richly textured piece of infrastructure – provides the entrance to the park, the armature for an 'invisible' glass hall behind and the backdrop to an egg-shaped pavilion.

Passing through the entrance, visitors find themselves in a generous double-height transparent space, which connects them visually to the open-air museum. In the glazed wall facing the park, the suppression of horizontal joints and the use of irregularly spaced vertical timber mullions distances the construction from the rational grid and aligns it more sympathetically with the surrounding woods. As visitors walk inside the building, the timber mullions have the effect of opening and closing views of the meadow and the buildings that occupy the landscape.

The pavilion is mysterious. It appears to be inaccessible and its form is difficult to place among the historic buildings on display. It becomes the icon of the museum, but, in contrast with the idealized cone at Delft, its soft, complex contours and copper cladding make it ambiguous, suggesting figural and topographic qualities.

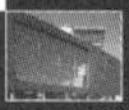

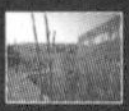

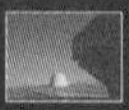

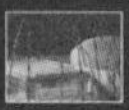

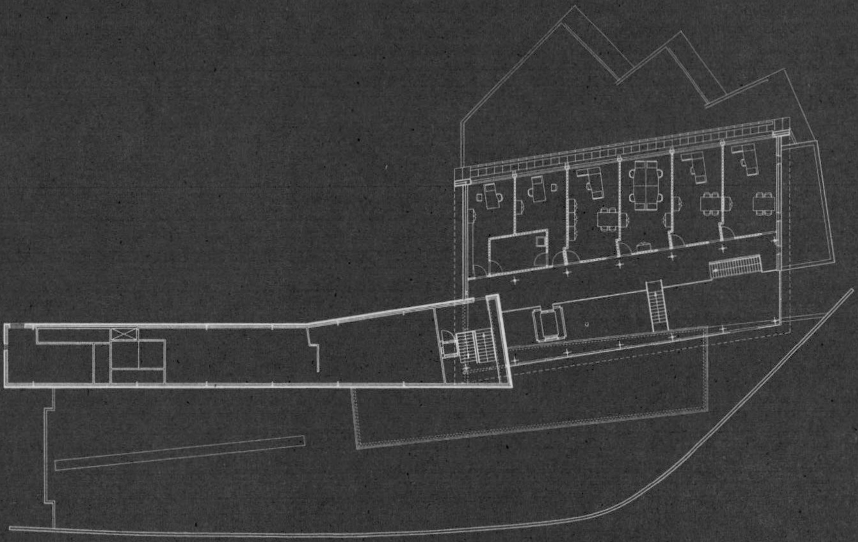

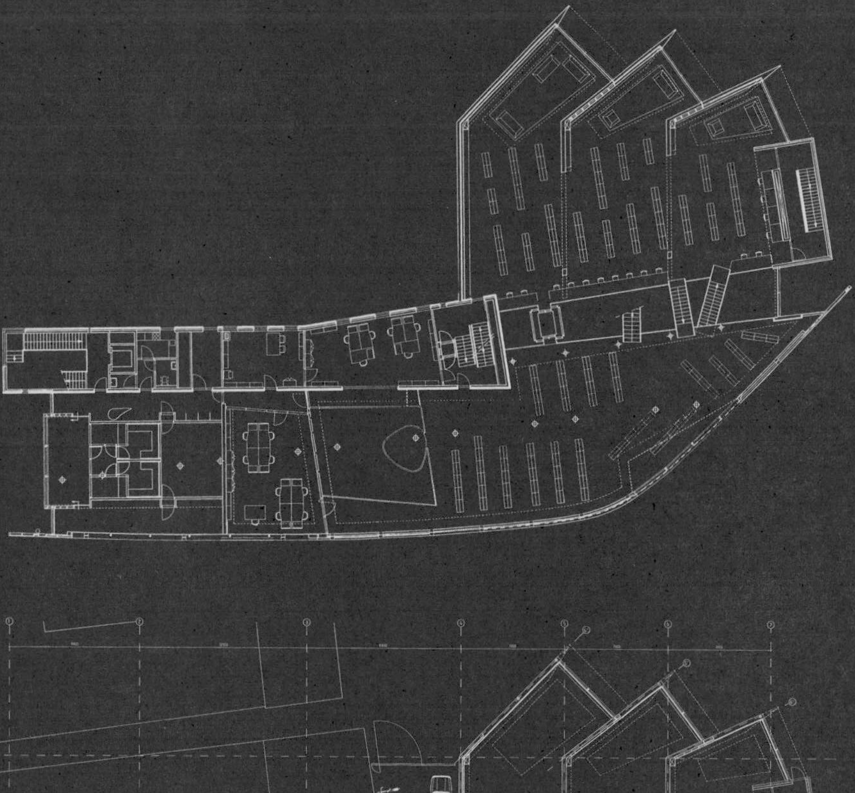

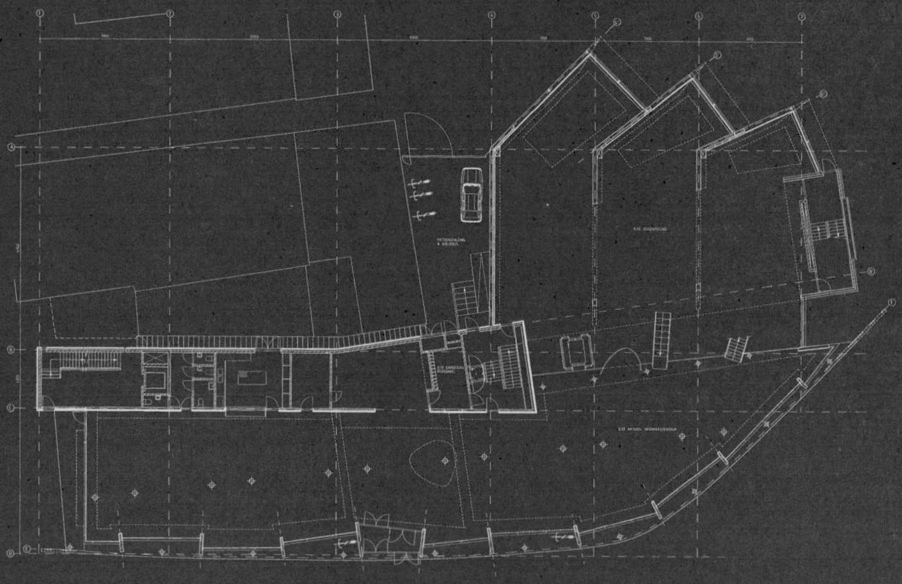

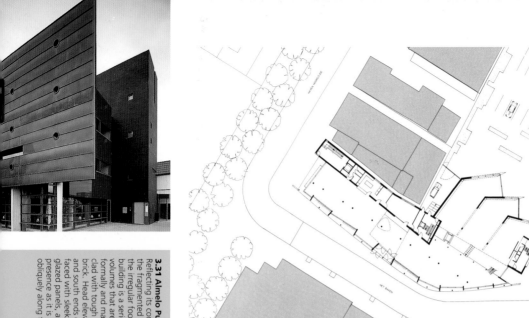

3.31 Almelo Public Library
Reflecting its complex programme, the fragmented urban context and the irregular footprint of the site, the building is a series of overlapping volumes that are distinguished formally and materially. The spine is clad with tough industrial black brick. Head elevations to the north and south ends of the building, faced with sleek ultramarine silicone-glazed panels, announce the library's presence as it is approached obliquely along the street.

Site plan

Exploded axonometric

3.31 Almelo Public Library
The glazed sawtooth façade of the reading café and information centre gives the library an extroverted commercial presence on the street. In contrast, the curved copper-clad façade of the upper floors emphasizes the more closed and introverted character of the library stacks. Internally, a playful and very public pulpit overlooking the entrance hall provides a counterpoint to the quiet, more private study areas between the concrete fin walls.

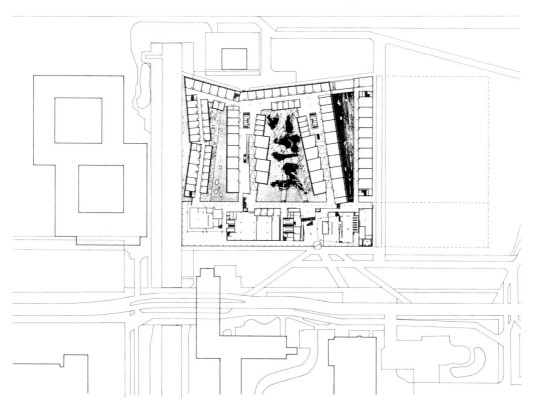

Site plan

Long section showing ramps and foot bridges

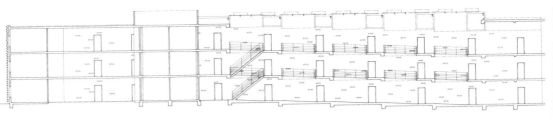

3.32 Faculty of Economics and Management

The building is located in the 'kasbah', an area of the university in which new amenities are concentrated, thereby creating a social focus for the commuter campus that was built in the 1960s. The lecture halls appear to float within a glazed bar facing the street. A restaurant overlooks the adjacent canal and, between the halls, a series of balconies become spaces for casual conversation, informal meetings and waiting areas between lectures.

3.32 Faculty of Economics and Management
Classrooms flank the central courtyard, with faculty and staff offices lining the outer courtyards and the perimeter of the building. Where corridors cross, the plan relaxes into an open 'square' for each discipline. The courtyards' theatrical landscapes combine with the interior topography to create a varied context for academic life.

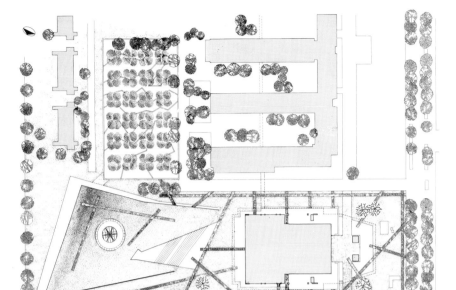

Site plan

3.33 Library, Delft University of Technology

Sited on a suburban campus designed in the 1960s, and adjacent to an enormous brutalist concrete assembly building, the new library is both landscape and landmark. The building's turf-covered roof, which is easily accessible for walking and lounging on, provides the campus with a new public space, while the the cone functions as a beacon.

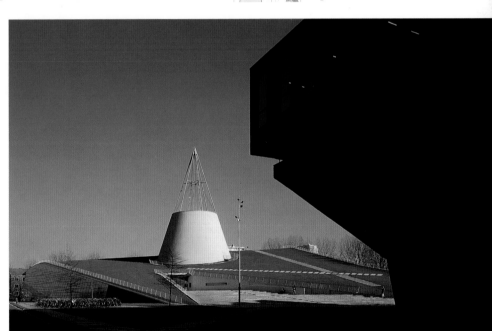

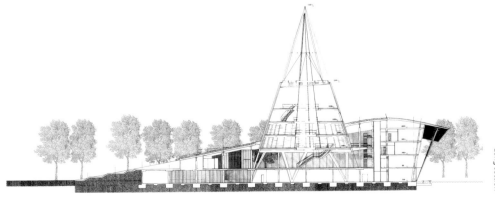

Long section

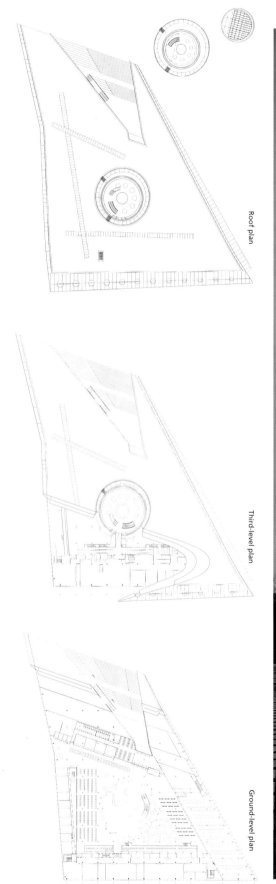

Roof plan

Third-level plan

Ground-level plan

3.33 Library, Delft University of Technology
The cant of the glazed façades and the horizontal mullions, which free themselves from the repetitive grid of the curtain wall to create an agitated pattern of dashed lines, help to detach roof from wall and enhance the illusion of a light, floating roof plane. The cone, an icon of the university's technological focus, appears to be a solid mass where it penetrates the roof, but turns into a skeletal frame at its apex.

3.33 Library, Delft University of Technology
The theme of weightlessness is emphasized at every opportunity. To avoid the large sections of steel that would be required if used in compression, the emblematic and extremely heavy tower of books hovers just 5.9 inches (15 cm) above the floor and is hung from the roof on 2.95-inch-diameter (7.5 cm) steel rods. The cone, washed with a necklace of daylight and supported on improbably slender steel columns, seems to float within the vast interior space.

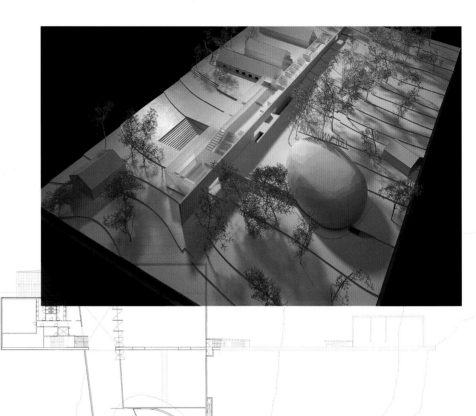

Basement-level plan

3.34 Dutch Open-Air Museum
An enormous wall that divides the open landscape from the museum park is a mosaic of bricks and traditional Dutch bonding patterns. Within the park, the new building houses a shop, café and information centre at ground level, while at basement level, a tunnel leads from exhibition galleries to a panoramic multimedia theatre in the copper-clad egg-shaped pavilion.

Ground-level plan

Sections

3.41

3.42

3.43

3.44

Patkau Architects
Heterogeneity

John and Patricia Patkau founded their practice in the late 1970s on the Canadian prairies, where the seemingly endless, flat landscape is defined by a rational grid of settlement. This grid, with its potential for infinite extension, endeavours to master nature through an idealized concept of space, and, as if responding intuitively to its consistent, over-arching order in the marking of the ground, the Patkaus' initial work was homogeneous in character. Migrating to the west coast of British Columbia in the early 1980s, they were – like many immigrants – acutely sensitive to their new environment. The wild and rugged landscapes bounded by the ocean at the edge of the continent have had a profound impact on their thinking. In lieu of the ideal, their work is increasingly focused upon the development of heterogeneity in response to the particular physical and cultural context of each project and as a means of investigating the complex and evolving relationship between man and nature.

This relationship is a fundamental preoccupation in Canada, a country where settlement patterns, and even prospects of survival, have historically been shaped by landscape and climate. These factors, combined with the overlay of European customs on aboriginal ways of life, have produced a culture of marked contrasts in a nation comprising vast tracts of virgin terrain, yet where the majority of people live in a handful of cosmopolitan cities strung along the southern border. In focusing on the relationship between nature and culture, the Patkaus explore this paradoxical Canadian condition and suggest that it is of universal relevance. Their work – perhaps because of the northern latitude and the pervasive landscape – has much in common with such Nordic architects as Alvar Aalto, Jørn Utzon and Sverre Fehn. It is preoccupied with the ground and grounding, and with the use of materials to generate an evocative tectonic language. Learning directly through building, the Patkaus' thinking has been shaped by a deep respect for the craft of construction, and the tectonic has consequently been a primary vehicle for developing the theoretical underpinning of their work.

The Patkaus characterize their working process as a series of 'investigations into the particular', which begins with a search for 'found potential', that is, for those aspects of a project that can generate a unique order shaped by circumstance. Found potential is discovered through close scrutiny of the physical, social and cultural topography of each project and through the critical consideration of typological precedent. A recurring strategy in their work is to identify elements that can be heightened formally, spatially and materially within the generic type to provide moments of architectural intensification in an otherwise banal context. Homogeneous ordering systems and predictable types are thus replaced by 'an irregularly, or unevenly developed plan with concentrations of energy in a neutral field'.[1] The Patkaus describe these concentrations of energy as totemic – a term derived from the Ojibwa and Cree words for the emblematic pole placed in front of the house to signify inhabitation – thereby endowing them with an iconic status linked to the primordial act of settlement.

The desire for heterogeneity, expressed through the topographic and totemic, becomes more explicit in two public buildings designed concurrently in response to quite different geographical and cultural contexts. For Seabird Island School (1988–91), designed for the First Nation Salish people who live in the Fraser River Valley in British Columbia, the found potential is located in the inhabitants – a community that suffered from the imposition of European culture and that consequently regarded the generic, orthogonal prefabricated schools issued to them by the government as instruments of cultural genocide. The programme for the new building is recast so that, in addition to being a school, it also becomes a community centre.

In seeking a different kind of order that is more sympathetic to the sensibilities of this community, the form of the new building suggests both zoomorphic and topographic associations. Rational and topographic systems are superimposed so that, while the underlying order of the plan is governed by a unifying orthogonal grid, an irregular envelope and highly differentiated sections generate a complex form and richly varied interior spaces. In addition to its allusive quality, the building responds to climate and context in a simple, direct way; the exterior envelope forms a protective shield against cold north winter winds and opens southward to admit sun and to provide an open, accessible face to the village. Against a backdrop of clad construction, the public porch is an exposed timber frame that evokes the traditional salmon-drying rack. Heterogeneity, expressed by the juxtaposition of opposites – orthogonal and topographic, open and closed, skin and frame – makes the building particular, an empathetic response to the needs and desires of the community.

While the vocabulary of the Canadian Clay and Glass Gallery (see p 104) is very different from Seabird Island, it is likewise grounded in the particular. Departing from the familiar typological precedent of the gallery as a series of introverted neutral white boxes, the building consists of spaces of distinct and differing tectonic character, which are firmly connected to views of the external world and changing conditions of daylight. The found potential emerges from the conceptual connection between the making of the building and the art it houses. Located in the city, the gallery draws its formal and material vocabulary from nearby warehouses, and within the resulting big-box industrial space, totemic elements are highly articulated formally and experientially. To convey their significance and to contrast with the explicit frame-and-skin vocabulary of the building itself, the totemic elements become stereotomic forms cast in concrete.

The spatial order of the Canadian Clay and Glass Gallery, defined by an open-ended series of layers, is reflected in the tectonic detail. The language of layering is inherently well-suited to standard North American construction practices, but, by peeling back layers to reveal what is normally hidden, the banal character of the wall and its linings is transformed. By contrasting the enduring monolithic character of the totemic elements with the suggestion of weathering and decay that is embodied in the enclosing wall, the building becomes a lyrical evocation of the way in which shelter is shaped by time and the processes of nature. The Patkaus observe, 'As surely as the forces of nature act upon our buildings, we work upon the natural world. Gravity, rain and snow, wind, changes in temperature, plant and animal life, all act to reduce buildings to their material constituents. At the same time, we work upon the natural world at both the relatively small scale of the building site as well as the relatively large scale of resource extraction, processing, manufacture and transportation. It is no longer clear whether anything is truly natural or truly man-made.'[2]

This growing sense of reciprocity is underlined in more recent projects. The Barnes House (see p 110) – shaped by considerations of near and far, earth and sky, figure and field – develops the concept of shelter as a focusing device for landscape and creates a deliberate ambiguity and interconnectedness between nature and culture. At Strawberry Vale School (see p 116), although classroom units recur in rational, repeated modules, subtle dislocations in plan and section free the building from the strict order of the grid to fit more naturally into the contours of the site. The figure is fragmented so that the building becomes more an extension of a topographical field of forces. The inflected ground plane signals the emergence of a more emphatic interest in the stereotomic as a counterpoint to the layering of the enclosing frame and skin. Although both frame and skin have become more highly differentiated as the Patkaus' work has developed, Strawberry Vale reiterates their constant underlying characterization of the frame as dynamic and clad construction as static. Yet, even within this opposition, many qualities are possible and, in contrast with the quiet, carefully resolved tectonic expression of the Barnes House, the language of Strawberry Vale is highly animated, like the children who inhabit the building.

The idea of erosion, closely related to the explicit layering of frame and skin, becomes increasingly important in the Patkaus' work, both as a mediator between building and landscape and as the means through which repetitive, generic spaces are made unique. Furthermore, at Strawberry Vale and in the project for the Nursing and Biomedical Sciences Building (see p 114), the evolving connection between building and nature expands from the formal and tectonic realms to become real. On a practical level, the notion of environmental sustainability affects the choice of materials, the design of structural and servicing systems and the detail of enclosure, which is responsive to climate. On a conceptual level, it provides the thread by which man and nature are inextricably connected.

In place of an abstract and idealized purity, Patkau Architects' work explores opposition, reconciling the objective with the subjective, and the generic with the particular. This conceptual investigation is supported by a tectonic language that searches for the extraordinary in the common everyday systems of building. Through conceptual and tectonic heterogeneity and the transformation of the seemingly banal into a finely nuanced poetry of construction, the Patkaus' architecture aspires to be grounded, that is, rooted in the contingencies of a complex and ambiguous world. In so doing, it is mindful of the proposition suggested by Vittorio Gregotti, 'Before transforming a support into a column, a roof into a tympanum, before placing stone on stone, man placed the stone on the ground to recognize a site in the midst of an unknown universe: in order to take account of it and modify it. As with every act of assessment this one required radical moves and apparent simplicity.'[3]

Notes
1   'Conversations with Patkau Architects', *Patkau Architects* (Halifax, Nova Scotia: TUNS Press, 1994) p 15.
2   *Investigations into the Particular*, The John Dinkeloo Memorial Lecture (Ann Arbor: College of Architecture + Urban Planning, University of Michigan, 1995) p 35.
3   Kenneth Frampton. *Studies in Tectonic Culture* (Cambridge, Massachusetts and London, England: The MIT Press, 1995) p 8. From an address by Vittorio Gregotti to the New York Architectural League in October 1982, published in *Section A1*, (no 1, February/March 1983) p 8.

3.4
Canadian Clay and Glass Gallery
Waterloo, Ontario, 1988–92

Located in a former industrial zone at the fringes of the city centre, the gallery comprises two large adjoining warehouse volumes that form the edge of a proposed new public space. A broad flight of steps leads up to a podium that defines the principal level of the gallery. A highly rational internal organization, with the entrance and all public facilities and offices on two floors in the east block, and double-height gallery spaces in the west block, is overlaid with a more expressive order of totemic elements. Each totemic element is an idealized form – circle, square or triangle – which is eroded and inflected in response to its particular use, orientation and connection to adjacent spaces and construction components. The small works gallery and the meeting room above it are profoundly introverted dark spaces deeply embedded in the plan. The courtyard, a void that ruptures the external envelope, allows the outer world to penetrate the body of the building. The stained-glass gallery is a positive figure, which breaks out beyond the confines of the enclosing wall. The fire columns, symbols of the transformative processes of making clay and glass, are free of the enclosure and become icons for the building, infusing the classical colonnade with a primal element of nature.

The construction reveals a clear hierarchy of heavy timber, steel framing and exposed concrete-block walls. To underline their importance, the totemic elements are made of reinforced concrete, the most difficult and enduring of building materials. In the courtyard, tile and wood veneers signify the invisible interstitial layers of the cavity wall and the absent formwork required to cast the concrete.

Barnes House
Nanaimo, British Columbia, 1991–93

3.42

Situated on a rocky outcrop with spectacular views across the Straits of Georgia to mainland British Columbia, the Barnes House is a mechanism through which the experience of place – from the immediate, small-scale textures of rock and trees to the distant expanse of sea – is intensified. Near the top of a hill, the house is sunk into a depression in the rock. Orthogonal and non-orthogonal geometries intersect. Plan and section are carefully calibrated to express the contrasting characters of excavated and constructed space; excavated walls, lined with storage units, are given an illusion of thickness, providing a counterpoint to the planar, free-standing façades. The ground-to-sky fissure in the external wall, like that of the Canadian Clay and Glass Gallery, breaks the box to draw people in at the lower level and to reconnect them with the world beyond on the upper level.

Materials are used to reveal their inherent qualities: the planar nature of light wood framing; the massive, compressive nature of concrete; and the linear, tensile nature of steel. Material expression, however, goes beyond the 'truth' of materials to suggest contrasts in character and representational attributes. The stuccoed wood-framed exterior wall is assertive on the south side of the house, which is in a clearing, while on the north side in the forest it becomes a weak and pliant form. Monolithic in character, the wall can be read as an extension of the rocky outcrop, while the folded roof, the three irregularly spaced columns – each a different height and diameter – and the leaflike steel canopy become built representations of the forest.

Nursing and Biomedical Sciences Building
The University of Texas, Houston, 1996–2000

3.43

The proposed building provides 250,000 square feet (23,212.6 square metres) of office, seminar, classroom and student-support facilities on a long, narrow site at the Texas Medical Center. The confined site and complex programme make a high-rise building inevitable. A generic shell is defined by clear span structure, flexible services and a demountable partition system. Within the shell, shared lounges, which are connected to adjacent floors by voids and open staircases and to the campus by exterior terraces, create an infrastructure for social interaction. In contrast with the generalized character of much of the programme, selected elements – the lobby, auditorium and dining room at ground level; the shared lounges and terraces on upper levels; and the rain-water storage tank, garden and dining rooms at roof level – provide moments of architectural intensification that produce a strong character and lasting identity for the building.

A multilayered building envelope merges structure and skin to form a weathertight enclosure, and uses a loose outer layer to temper the hot, humid climate. Protection from the sun is provided by a system of operable horizontal louvres on the east and west façades and a canopy above the roof. The canopy collects rain to supply non-potable water for the building and carries photovoltaic cells to power the ventilation and cooling systems. The form of the building maximizes the use of natural daylight, thereby reducing electrical running costs. Through its carefully tuned response to site and climate, the building seeks to create a symbiotic relationship between the health of the environment and the health of mankind.

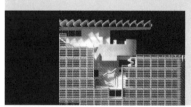

Strawberry Vale School
Victoria, British Columbia, 1992–96

3.4

Defining the boundary between settlement and nature, the school is shaped in response to the topography of the site. While the protective north façade, which faces a suburban neighbourhood, is frontal and figural, the south side of the building, which opens to and is penetrated by the landscape, becomes an extension of the rocky ground in a woodland of rare Gary oaks. Classrooms face the southern sun and views of the woods and, together with a library, computer room, special educational facilities and faculty offices, define a loosely ordered linear building that adjusts to accommodate the site's natural features.

Classrooms and communal facilities are linked by a route that replaces the institutional corridor with a meandering path. The path provides currents of movement, and branching off it are areas to pause for quiet conversation and a small amphitheatre for storytelling. While the stepped and ramped ground is carefully attuned to the contours of the site, the roof takes on a freer topographical character, generating highly differentiated interior spaces, ranging from the lofty circulation spine to intimate covered outdoor play areas between classrooms, where the deep overhanging eaves seem almost to touch the ground.

To avoid the harvesting of first-growth trees, steel is used for long structural spans and enclosure is provided by light wood framing. In such active areas as the gymnasium and the circulation spine, steel and wood framing are exposed and, together with the intersecting geometries of canted planes, generate complex, tactile surfaces amplified by strong patterns of light and shadow. In quieter areas, such as the classrooms, the frame is clad to create visually calm and luminous spaces.

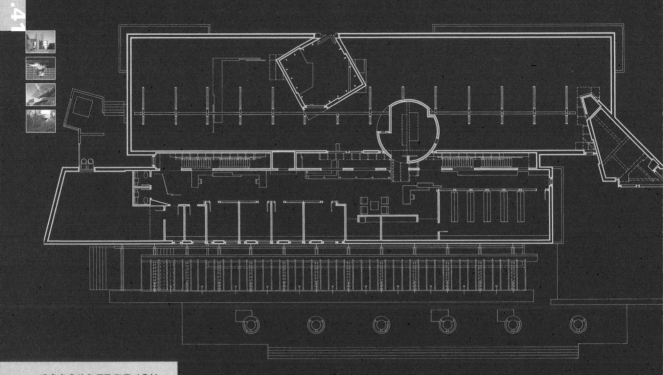

**3.41 Canadian Clay and
Glass Gallery**
The tectonic language of the
building breaks the box form
in a number of ways. The two
principal volumes are slipped
both relative to one another
and to the row of fire columns
so that no single axis of alignment
can be identified. Two corners
are wrapped by glazed bays while
a third is split open by the stained-
glass gallery.

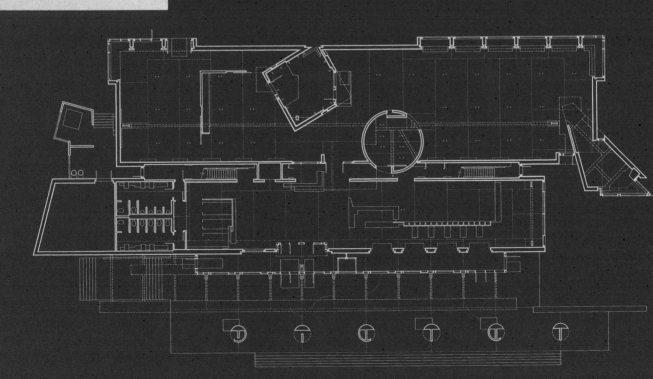

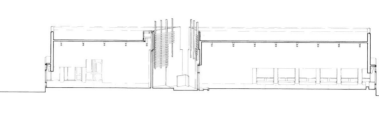

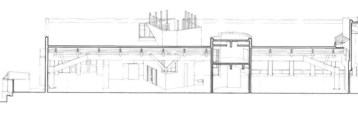

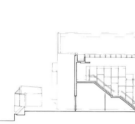

3.41 Canadian Clay and Glass Gallery

Vertical circulation is held between the building's layers, and structural elements reinforce the linear reading of the scheme. Rather than a rational grid of columns, a counter-intuitive deep longitudinal steel beam defines the gallery's vertical zone of space.

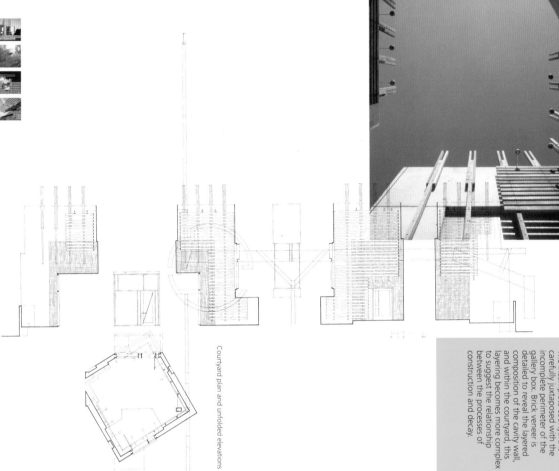

Courtyard plan and unfolded elevations

3.41 Canadian Clay and Glass Gallery

The incomplete courtyard is carefully juxtaposed with the incomplete perimeter of the gallery box. Brick veneer is detailed to reveal the layered composition of the cavity wall, and within the courtyard, this layering becomes more complex to suggest the relationship between the processes of construction and decay.

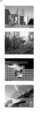

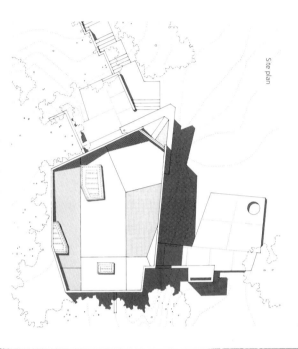

Site plan

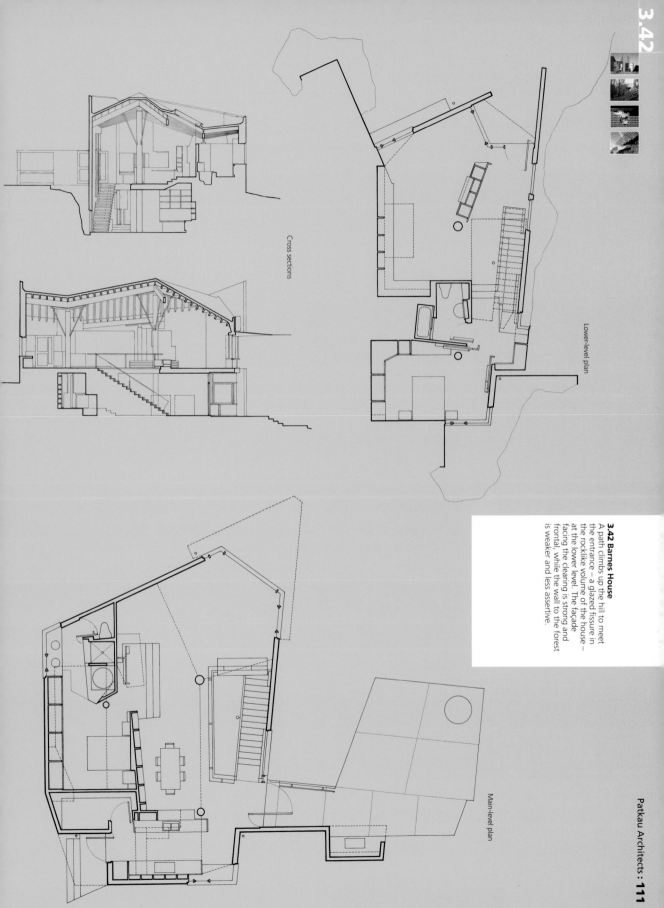

Cross sections

Lower-level plan

Main-level plan

3.42 Barnes House
A path climbs up the hill to meet
the entrance – a glazed fissure in
the rocklike volume of the house –
at the lower level. The façade
facing the clearing is strong and
frontal, while the wall to the forest
is weaker and less assertive.

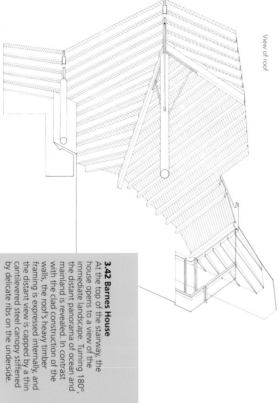

View of roof

3.42 Barnes House
At the top of the stairway, the house opens to a view of the immediate landscape. Turning 180°, the distant panorama of ocean and mainland is revealed. In contrast with the clad construction of the walls, the roof's heavy timber framing is expressed internally and the distant view is capped by a thin cantilevered steel canopy stiffened by delicate ribs on the underside.

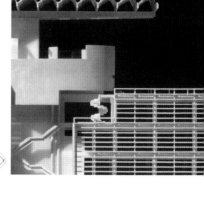

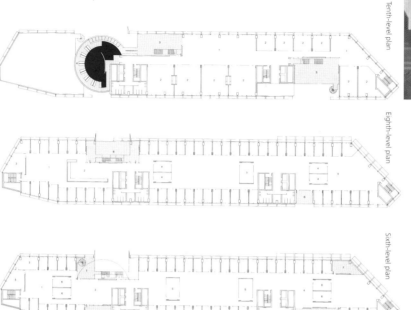

Tenth-level plan

Eighth-level plan

Sixth-level plan

A loose, variable outer skin and totemic 'organs' erode the generic building and develop a particular architectural character, as well as the attributes of a living creature. The building's design avoids the use of costly mechanical servicing, thus carrying the concept of reciprocity between man and nature to a much higher level of development, both technically and aesthetically.

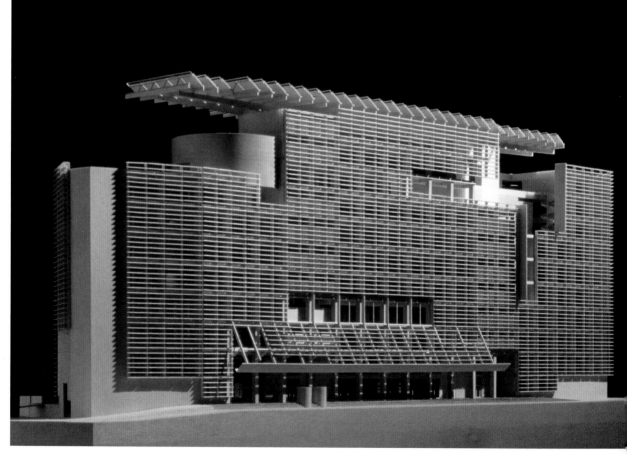

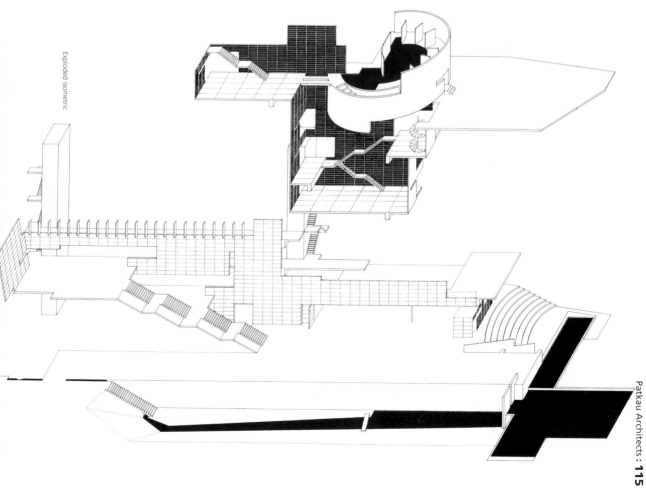

Exploded isometric

3.44 Strawberry Vale School
The building reflects and amplifies the topography of the site. Repetitive clusters of classrooms shift in plan to fit between groups of rocks and trees. The interior spaces are held between the stereotomic floor plane, which steps to the contours of the ground, and the more exaggerated topography of the skin-and-frame enclosure.

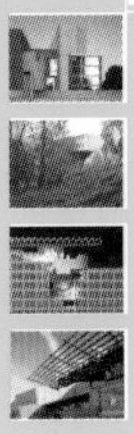

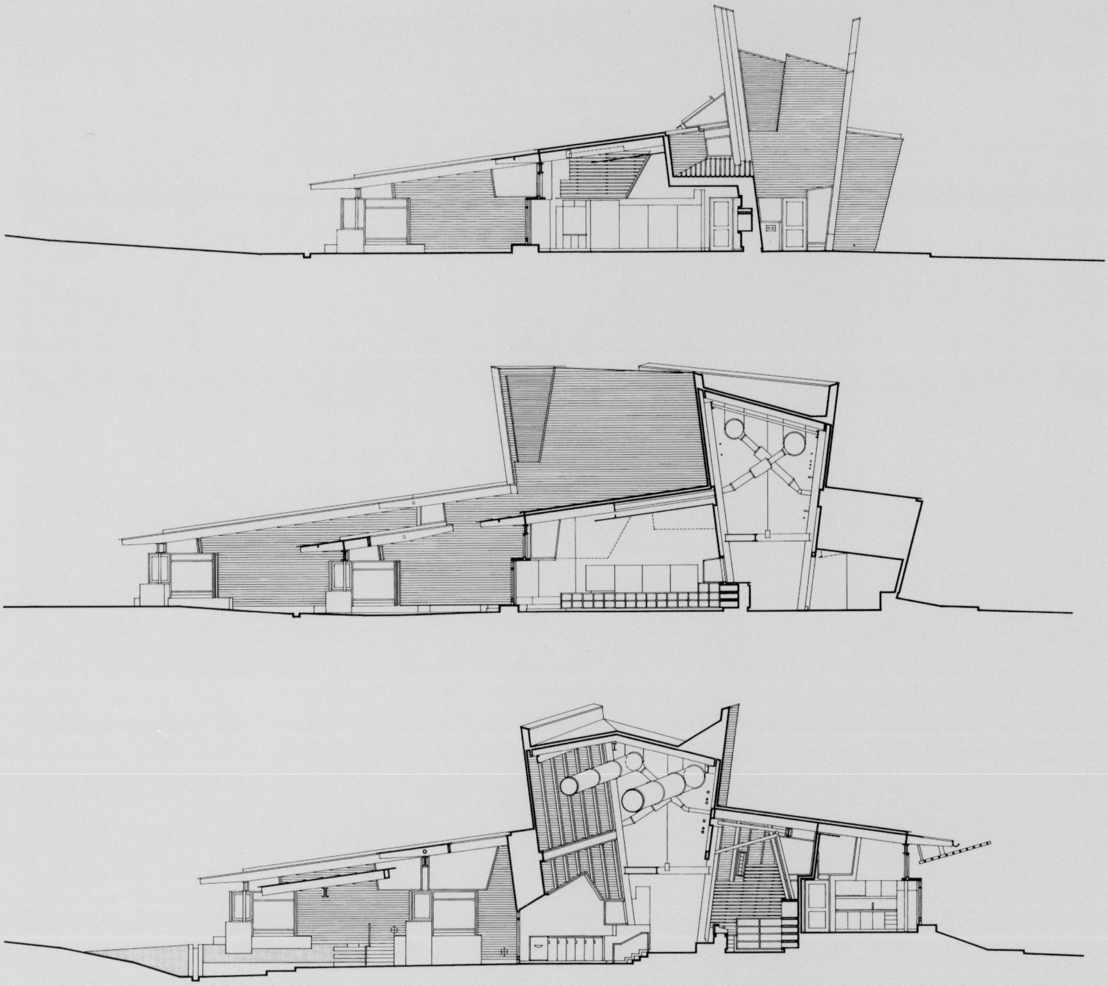

Cross sections

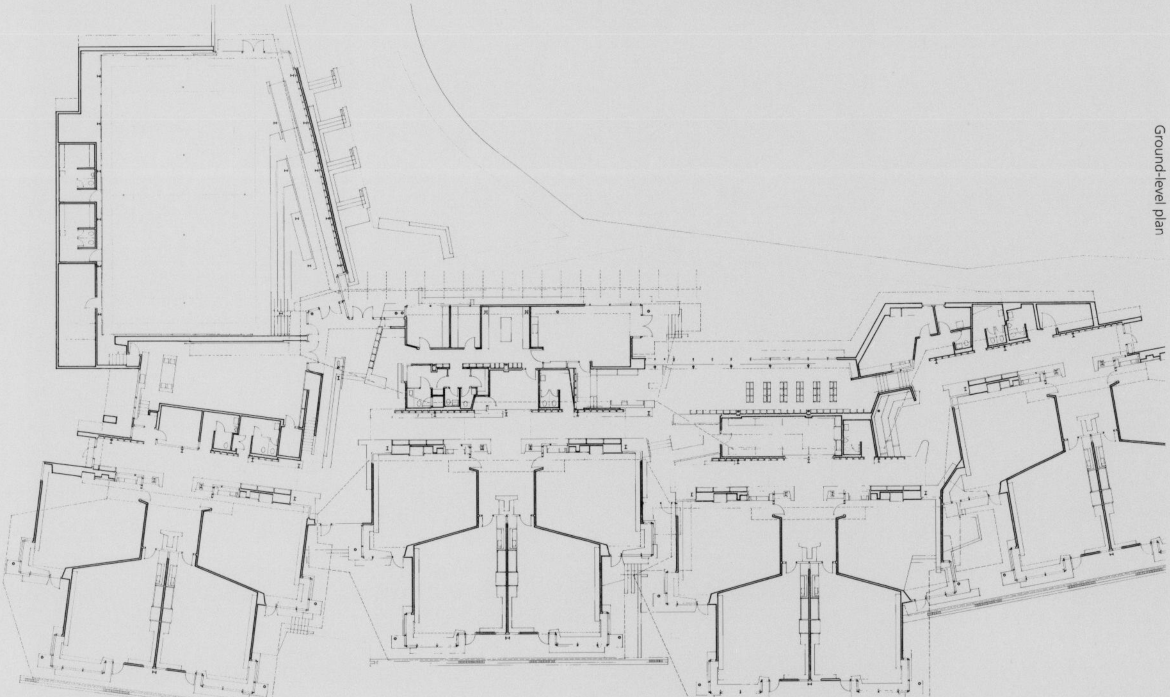

Ground-level plan

3.44 Strawberry Vale School

Expressed construction activates the circulation spine of the building, while clad construction creates a calm atmosphere in the classrooms. In addition, the exposure of materials and structure and the articulation of the layers of enclosure is didactic, helping to teach children how buildings shelter man from nature.

Roof plan

3.44 Strawberry Vale School
White-painted gypsum board is cut away to admit light from the tall circulation spine and to reveal the framing of intimate transitional porches at the low, outer edges of the classrooms, which focus on close views of the landscape. Layers are also revealed externally, with the thick insulated standing-seam steel roof giving way to the thin, flat-seamed cladding on the uninsulated eaves.

Enric Miralles

Biographical notes

Enric Miralles Moya received his architecture degree in 1978 from the Escuela Tecnica Superior de Arquitectura in Barcelona and was awarded a doctorate there in 1981. He opened a studio in Barcelona in 1984 where he worked in partnership with Benedetta Tagliabue until his death in 2000. Miralles's previous partnerships were with Helio Piñon and Albert Viaplana (1973–85) and Carme Pinós (1984–89).

Miralles was a Fulbright visiting scholar at Columbia University in 1981. He had been a professor in the Escuela Tecnica Superior de Arquitectura in Barcelona since 1985 and had directed a master's course at Frankfurt's Städelschule since 1990. He was a professor at Harvard University, where his first position was the Kenzo Tange Chair from 1992 to 1993. He also held the J. Labatut Chair at Princeton University between 1993 and 1994. Miralles taught and lectured at numerous architecture schools in Europe and the United States, including the Architectural Association in London, the Berlage Institute in Amsterdam and the Mackintosh School in Glasgow.

In addition to projects in Spain, Miralles completed buildings in Japan, the Netherlands and Germany. The office won international competitions for the Music School in Hamburg, the new Scottish Parliament in Edinburgh and the Instituto Universitario di Architettura (IUAV) in Venice.

Among other awards, Miralles received the FAD Prize in 1985 for La Llauna School and in 1992 for Igualada Cemetery; the Barcelona City Prize in 1992 for the Olympic Archery Ranges; the Madrid City Prize in 1993 for the Circulo Lectores; and the National Prize for Spanish Architecture in 1996 for Morella School.

Select bibliography
Monographs

Tagliabue, Benedetta, Enric Miralles and Thomas Bayrle. *Watering* (Frankfurt: Jurgen Hausser, 1999).

Zabalbeascoa, Anatxu and Javier Rodriguez Marcos, eds. *Miralles Tagliabue: Time Architecture/Arquitecturas del Tiempo* (Barcelona: Gustavo Gili, 1999).

Tagliabue Miralles, Benedetta, ed. *Enric Miralles: Works and Projects 1975–1995* (New York: The Monacelli Press, 1996).

Zabalbeascoa, Anatxu. *Igualada Cemetery: Enric Miralles and Carme Pinós* (London: Phaidon Press Limited, 1996).

Blundell Jones, Peter. *Enric Miralles: C.N.A.R. Alicante* (Stuttgart: Axel Menges, 1995).

Miralles, Enric and Alejandro Zaera. 'Enric Miralles: 1995'. *El Croquis* (no. 72, part 2, 1995).

Tagliabue, Benedetta, ed. *Enric Miralles: Mixed Talks*, Architectural Monographs (no. 40, London: Academy Editions, 1995).

'Enric Miralles, Carme Pinós, 1983–1994: Built Works'. *El Croquis* (nos. 30, 49–50, 1994).

Rigillo, Marina. *Miralles/Pinós. Architettura tra artificio e natura: progetti dal 1984 al 1990* (Rome: Gangemi, 1994).

'Enric Miralles, Carme Pinós: En Construccion/Under Construction'. *El Croquis* (no. 49–50, June–September 1991).

Montaner, Joseph María. 'Miralles, Pinós: Works and Projects 1984–1987'. *El Croquis* (no. 30, October 1987).

Articles/Features

Futagawa, Yukio. 'Enric Miralles. National Centre for Rhythmic Gymnastics, Alicante, Spain; Civic Centre Hostalets, near Barcelona, Spain'. *GA Document* (no. 38, 1994): 72–97.

Zucchi, Cino and Chiara Scortecci, eds. 'Construction'. Lecture by Enric Miralles transcribed in *Bau Kunst Bau* (Milan: Clean Edition, 1994): 66–83.

Futagawa, Yukio. 'Enric Miralles/Carme Pinós. Archery Range Facilities. Valle de Hebrón, Barcelona Spain.' *GA Document* (March 1992): 50–79.

Project information

Igualada Cemetery 1985–96

Architects: Enric Miralles, Carme Pinós
Building direction: Enric Miralles
Project team: Joan Callis, Se Duch, Albert Ferré, Josep Miàs, Eva Prats
Photography: Hisao Suzuki, Annette LeCuyer

Archery Ranges 1989–92

Architects: Enric Miralles, Carme Pinós
Building direction: Enric Miralles, Silvia Martinez
Project team: Albert Ferré, Eva Prats, Rodrigo Prats
Photography: Hisao Suzuki

National Training Centre for Rhythmic Gymnastics 1989–93

Architects, initial project: Enric Miralles, Carme Pinós
Architects, final project: Enric Miralles, Josep Miàs
Building direction: Enric Miralles, Josep Miàs
Project team: Iñaki Baquero, Cessare Battelli, Josep Bohigas, Peter Bundgaard, Joan Callis, Ricardo Flores, Miquel Lluch, Byarne Mastenbroek, Josep Miàs, Francesc Pla, Eva Prats, Rodrigo Prats, Josep Ustrell, Inken Witt, Pia Wortham
Photography: Domi Mora

Scottish Parliament 1997–2002

Associate architects: Enric Miralles, Benedetta Tagliabue
Collaborators: RMJM Scotland Ltd., Mike Duncan, Brian Stewart (directors)
Competition team: Joan Callis (project leader), Omer Arbel, Fabian Asunción, Steven Bacaus, Constanza Chara, Michael Eichhorn, Leonardo Giovanozzi, Annie Marcela Henao, Christopher Hitz, Ricardo Jimenez, Fergus McArdle, Francesco Mozzati
Project team: Joan Callis (project leader), Fabian Asunción, Sania Belli, Angel Caspado, Constanza Chara, Michael Eichhorn, Leonardo Giovannozzi, Sara Hay, Annie Marcela Henao, Michael Coing Maillet, Fergus McArdle, Umberto Viotto Nicoletti, Nadja Pröwer, Bernardo Ríos, Marco Santini, Gustavo Silva, Pedro Ogesto Vallina, Andrew Vrana
Photography: Lourdes Jansana

Günter Behnisch

Biographical notes

Born in Dresden in 1922, Günter Behnisch graduated from Stuttgart's Technische Hochschule in 1951 and opened his office in Sillenbuch in 1952. Since 1966, he has worked under the title Behnisch & Partners with Fritz Auer and Carlo Weber (until 1979), Winfried Büxel (until 1992), Erhard Tränkner (until 1993), and currently with Manfred Sabatke and senior architect Christian Kandzia. In 1989 Behnisch opened a second office in Stuttgart, where he was joined by Stefan Behnisch in 1992 and Günther Schaller in 1997. This office is known as Behnisch, Behnisch & Partner.

Behnisch was Professor for Design, Industrial Buildings and Planning and Director of the Institute for Building Standardisation at the Technical University in Darmstadt from 1967 to 1987, and in 1984 he was awarded an honorary doctorate from Stuttgart University. He was named Professor at the International Academy of Architecture in Sofia in 1991, and Honorary Professor at the Technical University of Karlsruhe in 1993.

In 1982, Günter Behnisch was elected as a member of the Akademie der Künste Berlin-Brandenburg. He was awarded the Gold Medal of the Academy of Architecture in France in 1992, and the Order of Merit for the Federal Republic of Germany in 1997. He is an honorary member of the Royal Incorporation of Architects in Scotland and the Royal Institute of British Architects.

The office has received numerous awards in Germany and internationally, including the Auguste Perret Prize of the International UIA in 1981 for the buildings and grounds of the 1972 Munich Olympics. The practice has also been nominated for the Mies van der Rohe Pavilion Award for European Architecture for the regional headquarters of the Diakonisches Werk in 1984, the Hysolar Institute in 1988, the Post and Communications Museum in 1990 and the Plenary Complex for the German Bundestag in 1992.

Select bibliography
Monographs

Blundell Jones, Peter. *Günter Behnisch* (Basel, Berlin, Boston: Birkhäuser Verlag, 2000).

Günter Behnisch, Behnisch & Partners, Behnisch Behnisch & Partners. Introduction by John Reynolds (Seoul: Korean Architects, 2000).

Biscogli, Luigi. *Günter Behnisch: poetica situazionale* (Turin: Testo & Immagine, 1998).

Gauzin-Müller, Dominique. *Behnisch & Partners: 50 Years of Architecture* (London: Academy Editions, 1997).

Kandzia, Christian, ed. *Behnisch & Partner, Bauten und Projekte 1987–1997* (Stuttgart: Verlag Gerd Hatje, 1997).

'Günter Behnisch'. *Korean Architects* (no. 146, October 1996).

Deutscher Bundestag. Neuer Plenarbereich. Acht Fotografen sehen den neuen Plenarbereich des Deutschen Bundestags in Bonn (Heidelberg: Edition Braus, 1996).

Nakamura, Toshio. 'Günter Behnisch, Behnisch & Partners: Recent Works'. *Architecture + Urbanism* (no. 291, December 1994).

Vebele, Andreas and Sigrid Hansjosten. *A Walk Through the Exhibition: Behnisch & Partners* (Stuttgart: Verlag Gerd Hatje, 1993).

Vebele, Andreas et al. *Über das Farbliche – On Colour* (Stuttgart: Verlag Gerd Hatje, 1993).

Schmidt, Johann-Karl and Ursula Zeller. *Behnisch & Partner – Bauten 1952–1992* (Stuttgart: Verlag Gerd Hatje, 1992).

Nakamura, Toshio. 'Special Feature: Günter Behnisch'. *Architecture + Urbanism* (no. 236, May 1990).

Kandzia, Christian, ed. *Behnisch & Partner, Designs 1952–1987* (Stuttgart: Edition Cantz, 1987).

Klotz, Heinrich. *Architektur in der Bundesrepublik, Gespräche mit Günter Behnisch* (Frankfurt/Main, Berlin, Vienna: Verlag Ullstein, 1977).

Nakamura, Toshio. 'Behnisch and Partners'. *Architecture + Urbanism* (September 1973).

Harbeke, Carl-Heinz and Christian Kandzia. *Bauten für Olympia 1972* (Munich: Harbeke Verlag, 1972).

Articles/Features

Futagawa, Yukio. 'Special School: Albert Schweitzer-Schule'. *GA Document 34* (September 1992): 88–97.

Project information

Albert Schweitzer School 1987–91

Architect:	Behnisch & Partners
Project architect:	Wolfgang Hinkfoth
Site supervision:	Werner Eberle, Martin Hühn, Jürgen Mattman
Photography:	Christian Kandzia/Behnisch & Partner

Plenary Complex for the German Bundestag 1982–92

Architect:	Behnisch & Partners
Partners:	Günter Behnisch, Winfried Büxel, Manfred Sabatke, Erhard Tränkner
Project partner:	Gerald Staib
Project architects:	Matthias Burkart, Hubert Eilers, Eberhard Pritzer, Alexander von Salmuth, Ernst-Ulrich Tillmanns
Project team:	Arnold Ehrhardt, Steffi Georg, Bernd Linder, Falk Petry, Jürgen Steffens, Alexander von Padberg
Staff:	Till-Markus Bauer, Simon Eisinger, Ralph Helmer, Armin Kammer, Susan Kayser, Götz Klieber, Dieter Kowalczik, Achim Kulla, Ansgar Lamott, Bettina Maier, Eckard Mauch, Carmen Müller, Martina Nadansky, Anke Pfudel, Rolf Scheddel-Mohr, Kay von Scholley, Martin Volz, Matthias Wichmann, Carola Wiese, Jens Wittfoht
Collaborator:	Christian Kandzia
Site supervision:	Ulrich Liebert, Heinz Schröder, Bernd Troske

Site staff:	Gabriele Hartmann, Peter Kling, Kai Kniesel, Karl Soboll
Photography:	Christian Kandzia/Behnisch & Partner

State Insurance Building, Schleswig-Holstein 1992–97

Architect:	Behnisch, Behnisch & Partner
Partners:	Günter Behnisch, Stefan Behnisch, Günther Schaller
Project leader:	Gunnar Ramsfjell
Project architects:	Martin Arvidsson, Birger Bhandary, David Cook, Jörn Genkel, Martin Gremmel, Horst Müller, Martina Schaab, Jörg Usinger
Project team:	Elke Altenburger, Thomas Balke, Marc Benz, Iris Bulla, Kathrin Dennig, Stefan Forrer, Jutta Fritsch, Pietro Graniola, Heiko Krampe, Cecilia Perez, Timo Saller, Matthias Schmidt, Jan Soltau, Georg Taxhet, Karin Weigang
Collaborator:	Christian Kandzia
Site supervision:	Behnisch & Behnisch, Büro Innenstadt (Stuttgart), Cronauer Beratung + Planung (Munich), Bernd Giesen (CBP), Axel Bruchmann, Heiko Krampe, Ulrich Jedelhauser
Photography:	Christian Kandzia/Behnisch & Partner

Harbourside Centre for the Performing Arts 1996–98

Architect:	Behnisch, Behnisch & Partner
Partners:	Günter Behnisch, Stefan Behnisch, Günther Schaller
Project partner:	David Cook
Project team:	Martin Arvidsson, Volker Biermann, Andreas Ditschuneit, Martin Gremmel, Jill Hauck-Spaeh, Malte Hofmeister, Diana Michael, Frank Ockert, Klaus Schwägerl, Ian Waters
Photography:	Christian Kandzia/Behnisch & Partner

Mecanoo

Biographical notes

The early work of Mecanoo, founded in 1983 in Delft, focused upon the successful use of social-housing projects to regenerate difficult urban sites. Today, directed by partners Henk Döll and Francine Houben, the practice's work has expanded to include complex, multifunctional buildings and integral urban developments combining architecture, urban planning, landscape and infrastructure.

Henk Döll graduated from Delft University of Technology in 1984. He has lectured throughout Europe, Canada and the United States, and has taught at Delft, the Berlage Institute and the Academy of Architecture in Amsterdam. During 1994, he taught in Barcelona and in 1995, he was a visiting professor at Vienna Technical University.

Francine Houben graduated from Delft Technical University in 1984. She has lectured in Japan, Canada, the United States and throughout Europe, and has taught at the Berlage Institute and the University of Pennsylvania. From 1989 to 1995, she served on the board of the Netherlands Architecture Institute in Rotterdam, and in 1997 she joined The Council for Housing, Spatial Planning and the Environment as an advisor to the Dutch government.

Mecanoo won the prestigious Rotterdam-Maaskant Prize for Young Architects in 1987. In 1996, the Dutch Ministry of Education, Culture and Science awarded the Scholenbouwprijs to the practice for Isala School, and the Faculty of Economics and Management was nominated for the Mies van der Rohe Pavilion Award for European Architecture.

Select bibliography

Monographs

LeCuyer, Annette, ed. *Mecanoo: Selected Projects 1994–1999*, MAP 6 (Ann Arbor: University of Michigan, College of Architecture + Urban Planning, 1999).

Houben, Francine, Piet Vollaard and Leo Waaigers. *Mecanoo Architecten: Bibliotheek Technische Universiteit Delft* (Rotterdam: Uitgeverij 010, 1998).

Somer, Kees. *Mecanoo* (Rotterdam: Uitgeverij 010, 1995).

Rood, Lydia and Natalia Torella Prat, eds. *Mecanoo Architekten* (Madrid: Fundacion cultural del colegio de arquitectos de Madrid, Ediciones Pronaos, 1994).

Cusveller, Sjoerd, ed. *Mecanoo, Vijfentwintig Werken* (Rotterdam: Uitgeverij 010, 1987).

Articles/Features

Lootsma, Bart. 'University Library, Delft, The Netherlands'. *Domus* (February 1999): 22–29.

Futagawa, Yukio. 'Mecanoo. Library of the Delft University of Technology.' *GA Document* (June 1998): 90–103.

Van Assche, Peter. 'Frog Needs Grass'. *Bauwelt* (April 1998): 752–57.

'Mecanoo. Faculty of Economics and Management, Utrecht Polytechnic, The Netherlands, 1991–1995'. *Architecture + Urbanism* (September 1996): 20–35.

Futagawa, Yukio. 'Mecanoo: Faculty for Economy and Management, Utrecht Polytechnic. Public Library, Almelo'. *GA Document* (December 1995): 66–91.

Steiber, Nancy. 'Modern Departures'. *Progressive Architecture* (June 1995): 96–101.

Zevi, Luca. 'Mecanoo'. *L'architettura* (December 1994): 854–72.

Gazzaniga, Luca. 'Mecanoo Quartierre Prinsenland, Rotterdam'. *Domus* (January 1993): 38-47.

Van Toorn, Roemer. 'Architectuur om de Architectuur: Modernisme als Ornament in het Recente Werk van Mecanoo'. *Archis* (November 1992): 25–31.

Van Dijk, Hans. 'Pays-Bas. Nuages sur la tradition moderne.' *L'Architecture d'Aujourd'hui* (December 1989): 116–266.

Döll, Henk and Charlotte Maas, eds. *Komposities voor Stad en Woning* (Groningen: Gemeente Groningen, 1989).

Project information

Almelo Public Library 1991–94

Project team: Jan Bekkering, Joanna Cleary, Henk Döll, Aart Fransen, Renske Groenewoldt, Leen Kooman, Alexandre Lamboley, Maartje Lammers, Miranda Nieboer, William Richards, Anne-Marie van der Meer, Toon de Wilde

Photography: Christian Richters

Faculty of Economics and Management 1991–95

Project team: Monica Adams, Marjolijn Adriaansche, Carlo Bevers, Giuseppina Borri, Henk Bouwer, Gerrit Bras, Ard Buijsen, Birgit de Bruin, Nathalie de Vries, Chris de Weijer, Annemiek Diekman, Henk Döll, Aart Fransen, Francine Houben, Harry Kurzhals, Miranda Nieboer, William Richards, Mechtild Stuhlmacher, Katja van Dalen, Erick van Egeraat, Wim van Zijl

Photography: Christian Richters

Library, Delft University of Technology 1992–97

Project team: Monica Adams, Marjolijn Adriaansche, Jan Bekkering, Carlo Bevers, Henk Bouwer, Gerrit Bras, Ard Buijsen, Birgit de Bruin, Chris de Weijer, Annemiek Diekman, Ineke Dubbledam, Aart Fransen, Francine Houben, Alfa Hügelmann, Axel Koschany, Theo Kupers, Maartje Lammers, Paul Martin Lied, Bas Streppel, Katja van Dalen, Erick van Egeraat, Astrid van Vliet

Photography: Christian Richters

Dutch Open-Air Museum 1998–2000

Project team: Michael Dax, Chris de Weijer, Patrick Eichhorn, Aart Fransen, Saskia Hebert, Francine Houben, Pascal Tetteroo, Michel Tombal

Photography: Pieter Vandermeer

Patkau Architects

Biographical notes

Founded by John and Patricia Patkau in Edmonton, Alberta in 1978, Patkau Architects moved to Vancouver, British Columbia in 1984. Michael Cunningham became an associate in 1992, and a partner in 1995.

John Patkau received a Master of Architecture from the University of Manitoba in 1972 and, upon graduation, was awarded the Royal Architectural Institute of Canada Medal. Patricia Patkau received a Master of Architecture from Yale University in 1978. She was an assistant professor at the University of California in Los Angeles from 1988 to 1990 and a visiting professor at Harvard in 1993. She is presently an associate professor at the University of British Columbia.

The Patkaus have taught, lectured or been guest critics at a number of universities in Canada, the United States and Europe, including the University of California in Los Angeles, the University of Michigan and the University of Pennsylvania. In 1995, they were jointly appointed Eliot Noyes Professor of Architecture at Harvard University and are both Fellows of the Royal Architectural Institute of Canada and the American Institute of Architects.

Michael Cunningham received a Master of Environmental Design from the University of Calgary in 1982 and, upon graduation, was awarded the Royal Architectural Institute of Canada Medal. In 1997, he received the Ronald J. Thom Award for Early Design Achievement from the Canada Council.

Patkau Architects has received seven Governor General's Medals, awarded by the Royal Architectural Institute of Canada and four Progressive Architecture Awards, among others. In 1986, the office won a national competition for the Canadian Clay and Glass Gallery, and in 1996, they came first in an international competition for the Nursing and Biomedical Sciences Building at the University of Texas in Houston. Patkau Architects was selected to represent Canada at the 1996 Venice Biennale.

Select bibliography

Monographs

Patkau Architects. Introduction by Andrew Gruft (Barcelona: Gustavo Gili, 1997).

Patkau, John. *Patkau Architects: Investigations into the Particular*. 1995 John Dinkeloo Memorial Lecture (Ann Arbor: University of Michigan, College of Architecture + Urban Planning, University of Michigan, 1995).

Carter, Brian, ed. *Patkau Architects: Selected Projects 1983–1993* (Halifax: TUNS Press, 1994).

———. *The Canadian Clay and Glass Gallery: The Act of Transformation* (Halifax: TUNS Press, 1992).

Articles/Features

Frampton, Kenneth, ed. Patricia Patkau lecture and discussion, *Technology, Place & Architecture: the Jerusalem Seminar in Architecture* (New York: Rizzoli, 1998): 94–117.

'Gebaute Topographie'. *Architektur Innenarchitektur Technischer Ausbau* (May 1997): 74–79.

Widder, Lynnette. 'Room Constituted by Topography on Vancouver Island'. *Daidalos,* (no. 63, March 1997): 116–21.

Wagner, George. 'Tectonic Lessons'. *Architecture* (February 1997): 82–91.

Frampton, Kenneth. 'Tecto-Totemic Form'. *Perspecta,* (no. 28, 1997): 180–89.

Isenstadt, Sandy. 'Spectacular Tectonics'. *ANY* (Architecture New York, no. 14, 1996): 44–47.

Fisher, Thomas. 'Design as a Form of Inquiry'. *Progressive Architecture* (September 1995): 52–61.

McMinn, John. 'An Evolving Language of Construction'. *Insite* (May 1995): 27–28.

Arpiaienen, Laura. 'Conversation with John Patkau'. *Arkkitehti* (February/March 1995): 38–43.

Frampton, Kenneth. 'L'America incognita: un'antologia/America Incognito: An Anthology'. *Casabella* (December 1993): 51,54,62–63, 70.

Gruft, Andrew. 'Analysis'. *A Measure of Consensus: Canadian Architecture in Transition* (Vancouver: UBC Fine Arts Gallery, 1986): 29–51.

Project information

Canadian Clay and Glass Gallery 1988–92

Associate architect:	Mark Musselman McIntyre Combe Inc.
Project team:	Michael Cunningham, Tony Griffin, John Patkau, Patricia Patkau, Tom Robertson, Peter Suter
Photography:	Steven Evans, Patkau Architects Inc, James Dow, William E Nassau

Barnes House 1991–93

Project team:	Tim Newton, John Patkau, Patricia Patkau, Tom Robertson, David Shone
Photography:	James Dow

Nursing and Biomedical Sciences Building 1996–2000

Project team:	Tom Bessai, Greg Boothroyd, Michael Cunningham, Maria Denegri, Joanne Gates, Jeff Gilliard, Felix Harbig, Julie La Freniere, Tim Newton, John Patkau, Patricia Patkau, Martin Schwarzenbach, Lydia Schymansky, David Shone, Peter Sturzenegger, Steve Suchy, Peter Suter, Jason Tang, Tamara Ulisko, Kevin Wharton, Sabine Wohlfahrt
Photography:	James Dow

Strawberry Vale School 1992–96

Project team:	Grace Cheung, Michael Cunningham, Tim Newton, John Patkau, Patricia Patkau, David Shone, Peter Suter, Allan Teramura, Jacqueline Wang
Photography:	James Dow

Illustration credits

(pp 1–23) **Frontmatter** p 1 Igualada Cemetery (Enric Miralles); p 2 Plenary Complex for the German Bundestag (Günter Behnisch); p 3 Albert Schweitzer School (Günter Behnisch); p 4 Library, Delft University of Technology (Mecanoo); p 5 Library, Delft University of Technology (Mecanoo); p 6 Strawberry Vale School (Patkau Architects); p 7 Canadian Clay and Glass Gallery (Patkau Architects); p 8 Archery Ranges (Enric Miralles). **Introduction** p 14 © Simo Rista; p 16 Christian Kandzia/Behnisch & Partner; p 19 © FLC/ADAGP, Paris and DACS, London 2001; p 20 Annette LeCuyer, © DACS 2001 [right]; p 21 © The Alvar Aalto Foundation; p 22 Christian Richters; p 23 © 2001 by R. Thomas Hille

Cover design: *background image* Almelo Public Library (Mecanoo, photograph by Christian Richters); *front, from left* Archery Ranges (photograph by Hisao Suzuki), Albert Schweitzer School (photograph by Christian Kandzia/Behnisch & Partner), Almelo Public Library (photograph by Christian Richters), Canadian Clay and Glass Gallery (photograph by Steven Evans); *back, from top* Igualada Cemetery (photograph by Hisao Suzuki), Albert Schweitzer School (photograph by Christian Kandzia/Behnisch & Partner), Library, Delft University of Technology (photograph by Christian Richters), Canadian Clay and Glass Gallery (photograph by Patkau Architects Inc); *back flap, from top* Archery Ranges (photograph by Hisao Suzuki), State Insurance Building, Schleswig-Holstein (photograph by Christian Kandzia/Behnisch & Partner), Library, Delft University of Technology (photograph by Christian Richters), Strawberry Vale School (photograph by James Dow); *inside cover, front* State Insurance Building, Schleswig-Holstein (Günter Behnisch, photograph by Christian Kandzia/Behnisch & Partner); *inside cover, back* Albert Schweitzer School (Günter Behnisch, photograph by Christian Kandzia/Behnisch & Partner)

First published in paperback in the United States of America in 2001 by Thames & Hudson Inc., 500 Fifth Avenue, New York, New York 10110

Library of Congress Catalog Card Number 00-107989
ISBN 0-500-28266-8

Printed and bound in China by Everbest Printing Co. Ltd.